UNDERSTANDING ATONEMENT

UNDERSTANDING ATONEMENT

Maybe it's time to rethink atonement without giving up Jesus

✝

Gary A. Fox

RESOURCE *Publications* · Eugene, Oregon

UNDERSTANDING ATONEMENT
Maybe It's Time to Rethink Atonement without Giving Up Jesus

Wipf & Stock
An Imprint of Wipf and Stock Publishers
199 W. 8th Ave., Suite 3
Eugene, OR 97401

www.wipfandstock.com

PAPERBACK ISBN: 978-1-5326-8833-1
HARDCOVER ISBN: 978-1-5326-8834-8
EBOOK ISBN: 978-1-5326-8835-5

Manufactured in the U.S.A.

For
Olivia Adell Chapman-Fox

My love for you is bigger than the universe.

Contents

Introduction
What Do You Think?

And forgive us our sins,
for we ourselves forgive everyone indebted to us.
—Luke 11:4a

Forgiveness is about love, not punishment. I said these words to two friends as we stood in the parking lot after church one Sunday. I said them because, just prior to this, I asked the question, "Why did Jesus die?" and they both responded, "For my sins." Then I asked them if they believed God loved them, and they both said yes.

"Is God's love for you based on Jesus's death, or simply because God is love and God loves you?" I asked. A puzzled look came over their faces. It was a question they had never considered. If God loves you, why would God need to punish Jesus for your sin? Then I said, "Forgiveness is about love, not punishment." And it was like a light bulb went off, and they both went, "Ohhhhhh." That's why I decided to write this book. I want to help people think through what we call atonement—why Jesus died.

I also wrote this because I want people to know they don't have to believe they are terrible, horrible sinners destined to hell if they don't accept Jesus as their substitute to bear the brunt of God's wrath. It seems weirdly illogical to say God is a God of love, but God will cast you into hell for all eternity to be tortured if you don't believe in Jesus.

I wrote this because when my daughter was born, she was born with methamphetamine and marijuana in her system. She is adopted and we had no control over what the birth mother did while pregnant. And it dawned on me one Sunday morning while teaching a parent Sunday school class: What if this predisposes her to addiction? So I asked the parents what they would do if their child developed some sort of addiction. The responses were mixed. I realized as I listened that, for me, it wouldn't matter. If my daughter got mixed up in drugs or even killed someone, I would never stop loving her. She would never stop being my child.

Jesus said, "If you then, who are evil, know how to give good gifts to your children, how much more will your Father in heaven give good things to those who ask him!" (Matt 7:11). Surely God is a better parent than I could ever be. So why would I believe that God could not even stand the sight of me because of sin? If I could accept my own daughter, no matter what she did, wouldn't God accept me? And the whole notion of atonement, where God needed a payment for wrongdoing, unraveled.

As I began to think about this more and more, it became a burning need to write. But I have to confess, what you hold in your hands is not a scholarly publication. I do not go into deep detail about each theory of atonement, nor do I try to cover every theory that has ever been proposed. I simply want to provide an easy-to-read overview that will cause you to think about what was going on when Jesus died and begin to ask the question, what does this mean for me and the world?

In chapter 1, we will look at what atonement means and how scripture doesn't necessarily support the need for it. Having said that, I want to point out that I have a high view of scripture and use it where I can to prove my ultimate point that we really don't need any atonement theories at all. In chapter 2, we will look at different theories of atonement throughout the 2,000 years of Christianity. In chapter 3, we will look at what the gospel means if it's not about Jesus dying in our place as a substitute to take on God's wrath.

This will lead nicely into chapter 4, what are God's wrath and judgment all about? Then comes my favorite chapter, chapter 5, the one I like to call "The Brain Chapter." It is about how our brain works and why we get attached to certain beliefs about God, the Bible, and atonement. In chapter 6, we will look at what the Old Testament has to say about atonement and the sacrificial system, as well as what Jewish people today believe about the purpose of atonement. Chapter 7 will cover what the New Testament says about atonement in the gospels, Paul's letters, and a few other New Testament books.

If you are wondering why it is even necessary to talk about the topic of atonement, I encourage you to read chapter 8. I call this "The Damage Chapter." The more widely understood theory of atonement in the West is what is called penal substitutionary atonement. Essentially this theory says that we owed a debt to God we could not pay because of sin. So God sent Jesus to pay our penalty and take on God's wrath in our place. For some people, this fear-based view of God has caused anxiety, and it has caused others to leave the church, even Christianity, altogether. That leads me to the final chapter, where do we go from here? If we are to do away with atonement altogether, what do we do with Jesus? What does it mean for Christianity and the future of the church? The interesting thing about the future of the church without a belief in atonement is that it is not that unrealistic. The idea that Jesus came to die for our sins, while professed by the majority of Christians, is not what they actually believe. Their profession does not match their belief. In 2015, the Pew Research Center conducted a survey regarding the beliefs of Americans on heaven and hell. Seventy-two percent of Americans believe in heaven as a place where people who have led good lives are eternally rewarded, and most Americans believe they will get there.[1] If 72 percent of Americans believe they are good enough to get into heaven, then why do they still say that Jesus died for their sin?

I hope that this book will help us understand that God loves us and will not forsake us. Period. Forgiveness is about love, not punishment.

---

1. Murphy, "Most Americans Believe," para. 1.

Chapter 1
What Is Atonement?

First, be reconciled to your brother or sister,
and then come and offer your gift.
—Matthew 5:24b

Our beliefs about God and the Bible change over time. When I was in seminary, we had to take a yearlong course called Systematics. The purpose was for us to think through what we believed about God, Jesus, the Holy Spirit, humanity, sin, salvation, the church, and the end times. Each section needed to be consistent with the others. Meaning, what you believed about humanity and sin had to logically flow into what you believed about salvation. For instance, if you believe that sin is genetic, that humanity is born sinful, then salvation must address this inherited sin problem. Our professor said we should rewrite our beliefs about these core Christian topics every ten years because they would not stay consistent over the course of our lives. He was right.

My own beliefs and convictions have changed drastically over the course of my lifetime as a Christian. Early on, particularly when I was in youth group in high school, my faith was shaped by friends and my youth pastor. In college, what I believed continued to be challenged and shaped by the Navigators Christian Fellowship group of which I was a part. The beliefs of my young adult professional years were shaped largely by a small group I attended and my church. I was very involved in church life and even worked a short while as a part-time youth pastor. So when I got to seminary at age 39, I felt like my faith and the systems I had built to support my belief were pretty rock solid. And then I took Christian history and my mind was truly blown.

Everything that I had believed was set in stone, I discovered had not always been the dominant view of the church in its history. For instance, I didn't realize that there were two distinct schools of thought—one Western and one Eastern. On the issue of sin, the Western thought was that sin was inherited; we were born sinful; it was genetic and passed down through Adam. But the Eastern church believed we were born innocent and eventually fell into the sin of Adam. Why hadn't anyone in all my years in church ever explained any of this to me? One issue I discovered that had varying views throughout church history was atonement.

If you believe sin is genetic, then salvation must address this birth defect, so to speak. And Jesus's role in taking care of that problem is called atonement. If you believe we eventually fall into the sin of Adam, then salvation is Jesus's work of forgiveness and a transformation of our hearts not to desire to sin anymore. Atonement is asking the question, how do we make things right with God for what we have done individually and as a human race due to sin?

The definition of atonement is to make reparations for wrongdoing, or repay someone or a group of people for a harm done to them. Governments do this all the time. Officials will often apologize on behalf of policies that led to discrimination, criminalization, and death of whole groups of people. In 1970, German Chancellor Willy Brandt fell to his knees at a commemoration of the Jewish victims of the Holocaust in the Warsaw Ghetto in Poland because words failed him. His action was a sign of utter humility and repentance in the face of a terrible wrong committed. The United States also has seen its fair share of wrongs committed against people groups. From the taking of land, human life, and dignity of the native peoples in America to the enslavement of Africans for purely economic reasons, the U.S. government has had to make reparations for wrongs we as Americans have committed. In many ways, these sins were committed because we have not loved our neighbors as ourselves.

This repeated pattern throughout human history of committing wrongs not only on a national level, but also on a personal level, is sin. Where we have not loved others as we love and care for ourselves, we have committed sin. The good news of the Christian message is that God forgives us so that we can live a new life of love for all people and all of God's creation. Christians for many centuries have seen this as a rebirth or renewal, even a recapturing of a deep inner feeling that this love is what God intended all along and that God is the source of this love, revealed perfectly in Jesus. In Psalm 36:7–8, the psalmist says of God's love, "How precious is your steadfast love, O God! All people take refuge in the shadow of your wings. They feast on the abundance of your house, and you give them drink from the river of your delights."

The psalmist declares that all people have refuge in God and access to God's abundance and delight. It is important to note that while this can be economic, it is also about dignity and the right of persons to be whole and live without fear. This is God's shalom, or God's perfect peace. It is salvation. Jesus came to affirm and demonstrate God's shalom by proclaiming the kingdom of God and God's way of being. In the beginning of the gospel of Mark, we find Jesus calling the disciples. Jesus chose the disciples to be closest to him and to learn from him about God's kingdom and God's way of being so that they could go out and do the same things Jesus did. God was not new to the first-century Jewish people. God had been their God for thousands of years. But Jesus was different from the religious teachers the people were used to. In Mark 1:22, it says that Jesus taught the people as someone who had authority, but not like the religious leaders of his day.

What was the primary difference between Jesus and the other religious teachers? I think it was that Jesus embodied what he taught—love. The religious leaders are portrayed as being very judgmental and tying up "heavy burdens, hard to bear, and lay[ing] them on the shoulders of others; but they [the religious leaders] themselves are unwilling to lift a finger to move them" (Matt 23:4). This indicates that Jesus's way of being, and then also God's way of being, was nonjudgmental. In short, people liked to be around Jesus. He made them feel good about themselves and feel that they were loved. Unfortunately, this is not the perception of God many seem to get from church today.

Diana Butler Bass, an author who often writes about the intersection of faith, politics, and religion, quoted a *Newsweek* report on two significant polls in American religion in her 2012 book *Christianity after Religion: The End of Church and the Birth of a New Spiritual Awakening*. In 1990, 86 percent of Americans identified as Christians.

In 2010, only 76 percent self-identified as Christians. During that same period, those claiming no religious affiliation doubled.[1] Bass offers a few reasons for this trend.

One, religion is seen as institutional, and what most people are looking for today is "spirituality" or something that is lively.[2] Two, the "horrible decade" happened. This is what Bass calls the "religious recession" at the dawn of the new millennium.[3] Several things happened that contributed to this religious recession. In 2001, the September 11 terrorist attacks occurred. After the first few months of a national resurgence in church attendance, the media and politicians began blaming the attacks on religious zealots of Islam, while some well-known Christian religious leaders like Pat Robertson, Jerry Falwell, and Franklin Graham blamed the attacks on homosexuals and feminists.[4] These leaders did not reflect the opinions of people seeking a connection to God in a very turbulent period in American life. Unfortunately, their positions harmed the church at a time when the church is increasingly seen as irrelevant.

In 2002, there was the Roman Catholic sex abuse scandal revealed by *The Boston Globe*. In 2003, there was the public Protestant debate over homosexuality with the election of Gene Robinson to an Episcopal Diocese. In 2004, George W. Bush's reelection was largely seen as accomplished because of his association with the religious right, a group seen as largely more interested in politics and promoting their own social agenda then witnessing to a God who cares deeply about people.[5] Bass says Christianity was viewed by young people as "anti-homosexual, judgmental, hypocritical, out of touch with reality, overly politicized, insensitive, exclusive, and dull."[6] This is not Bass's opinion. It is based on data collected in a Barna Group study on what sixteen-

---

1. Bass, *Christianity after Religion,* 13.

2. Bass, *Christianity after Religion,* 71.

3. Bass, *Christianity after Religion,* 77.

4. Bass, *Christianity after Religion,* 77.

5. While Bass's book was written before the 2016 elections, there is no argument now about the role the religious right played in the election of Donald Trump, which has soured even more people on Christianity. Trump's life and words reflect very little about concern for others, a tenet of the Christian faith.

6. Bass, *Christianity after Religion,* 81.

to-twenty-four-year-olds, within and outside the church, thought about Christianity.

The Barna Group study identified six broad themes believed about the church by this group: (1) it is hypocritical, appearing to only want those who are virtuous and morally pure, (2) it only cares about converts or getting people "saved," (3) it is anti-homosexual, (4) it is sheltered and out of touch with reality, (5) it is too political, and (6) it is judgmental, not caring about the attitudes and perspectives of others.[7] These perceptions are a far cry from the Jesus who made people feel loved and welcomed, even when no one else did.

I believe we are entering a time in church history when many of the things we were taught by the church leaders of our day are being challenged, questioned, and not simply taken at face value. Atonement is one of those things. The idea that God needed to send Jesus to die on a cross to satisfy God's need to punish sin is being questioned. The process of questioning things we once held to be true about our faith is called deconstruction. I recently was asked by my friend, Aaron Manes, what to do about atonement and the death of Jesus now that he has deconstructed his understanding that Jesus had to die for his sins. He didn't want to give up on Jesus, but he also could no longer believe in the idea that God sent Jesus to die for people's sins.

This is a good question. If we no longer believe Jesus had to die for our sins, but we love Jesus and the church, what do we do? First, let's look at the message of Jesus. What did Jesus say he came to do? In Mark 1:14–15, Jesus came to proclaim the good news of God, saying the kingdom of God was near, to repent, and to believe the good news. Then Jesus demonstrates the good news by healing people and casting out demons. I once heard a story about someone who had never been to church before, who was invited to attend a church home group. A person in the group mentioned the good news. The person who had never been to church asked, "What is the good news?" An explanation was offered that Jesus came to die for our sins because God needed a sacrifice to cover the sin. The person who had never been to church before began laughing. When he realized the person was serious, he asked, "How is that good news?"

---

7. Kinnaman and Lyons, *Unchristian*, 29–30.

Indeed.

The understanding of atonement presented in the home group is only good news if you fear punishment from God. But in Matthew 10:26–30, Jesus tells the disciples not to fear those who will persecute them and can destroy the body, but to fear the one who can destroy both body and soul in hell. Who is the one who can destroy both body and soul in hell? Is it God? Is it the devil? Jesus goes on to say that not even a sparrow falls from the sky without God knowing about it. Yet, we are much more important to God then sparrows. In fact, God knows exactly how many hairs are on our heads, "so do not be afraid" (Matt 10:31). Jesus says God cares about us and we are not to fear; God has our best interests at heart.

Our relationship with God is not to be based on fear. You may be thinking, what about the scripture that says, "The fear of the Lord is the beginning of knowledge . . ." (Prov 1:7), or perhaps, "It is a fearful thing to fall into the hands of the living God" (Heb 10:31)? And then there is 1 John 4:18: "There is no fear in love, but perfect love casts out fear; for fear has to do with punishment, and whoever fears has not reached perfection in love." Fear has to do with punishment. So which is it? Are we to fear God and God's punishing wrath, or not fear God because God is perfect love, which casts out fear?

The reality is we can find scripture to justify just about any position we want to take. There is no one way revealed in the Bible. The phrase "But the Bible says . . ." is actually true. The Bible says a lot of things and they don't all agree—even on the issue of atonement. So a question to consider as you read and contemplate atonement is this: How do I want to read and interpret scripture? Through a lens of fear or one of love?

In Mark 1:33, the whole city of Capernaum gathered at the door of Simon and Andrew where Jesus healed the sick and those with various diseases and cast out demons. The only ones expressing fear were the demons being cast out. The next day, Jesus goes out to pray early in the morning. His disciples go out looking for him and he tells them, "Let us go on to the neighboring towns, so that I may proclaim the message there also; for that is what I came out to do" (Mark 1:38). The only message he has proclaimed at this point in both Matthew 4:12–17 and Mark 1:14–15 is "Repent and believe the good news of God." In Luke 4:16–21, Jesus offers a little more by reading from the scroll of Isaiah where it says, "The Spirit of the Lord is upon me, because he has anointed me to bring good news to the poor. He has sent me to proclaim release to the captives and recovery of sight to the blind, to let the oppressed go free, to proclaim the year of the Lord's favor."

The Holy Spirit has commissioned Jesus to bring good news of restoration, healing, and freedom. Let's be clear. If anyone has anything to fear from this mission of the Holy Spirit, it is those who wish to control, manipulate, and keep people captive and sick. The goods news Jesus expressed and lived out was none other than love. Never once did Jesus say as part of his message, "I have come to die for your sins that you may have life eternally; otherwise, God will cast you into hell because you deserve to be punished." Yet, for many, this is what atonement has come to mean.

If you ask most Americans why Jesus died, they will say, "For my sins." It has become as commonplace as calling tissues Kleenex or a bandage a Band-Aid or a moving staircase an escalator. Wait, what? An escalator is an escalator. Actually in 1900, a company called Otis invented the moving staircase and trademarked the name Escalator. By 1930, the word was listed as an adjective to mean going up or down. By 1950, the name Escalator had become so commonplace it became part of the public lexicon and no longer was seen as a trademark. The same thing has happened with the question, why did Jesus have to die? People respond with "for my sins" without even thinking about it. But just because something has become commonplace, does not mean it's the truth or the only way to think about things.

To illustrate how commonplace this idea has become, if you look up the word "atonement" in the latest edition of the Merriam-Webster Dictionary, it provides two definitions. One is "the act of making amends for an offense or injury" and the second is "the reconciliation of God and humankind through the sacrificial death of Jesus Christ."[8] The literal definition of atonement in the dictionary is reconciliation of

---

8. *Merriam-Webster Online,* "atonement," accessed May 14, 2019, https://www.merriam-webster.com/dictionary/atonement.

humankind with God through Jesus's death. First, let's look at the word "reconciliation."

In the Merriam-Webster Dictionary, to reconcile means to restore friendship or harmony between factions, or to settle and resolve differences. In order for two parties to restore friendship or harmony, both parties must have agency. In social science, agency is the capacity of individuals to act independently and to make their own free choices. This means that in order for harmony to be restored between God and humanity, both must have the freedom, right, privilege, and ability to enter into that agreement. In many of the atonement theories, and particularly in substitution atonement, Jesus becomes the one who acts on our behalf. This may be beneficial in a court of law with a lawyer acting on your behalf, particularly in a situation where the two parties cannot come to an agreement, but what if the need to reconcile were between two friends?

Friendship with God seems to be the desire indicated in both the Old and the New Testament. In the Old Testament in 2 Chronicles 20:7 and in Isaiah 41:8, Abraham is referred to as God's friend. In Exodus 33:11, God speaks to Moses as friend. In the New Testament, Abraham is referred to as God's friend in James 2:23, and Jesus refers to Lazarus as "our friend" in John 11:11. Jesus refers to the disciples, and by extension to us, as friends in John 15:12–15, with the qualifier that we love one another. And that's what friendship is! It is a genuine love for one another. If a wrong is committed that damages the relationship, it is a recognition and admittance along with asking for forgiveness that restores the friendship. Requiring a blood sacrifice of death to restore that friendship would be, well, weird.

But what about those things that are so terrible, such as a gunman entering a school and shooting small children? A situation like this causes something to rise up within us and say, "That is unforgivable! No apology can make this right." In light of such terrible crimes, it is easier to say that we need an act of God to save us from ourselves. But the reality is, Jesus's death on the cross did not end the human bent toward harming others in word or deed. Jesus's death did not stop the consequences of our sin and the aftermath of pain that follows a tragedy.

Only forgiveness can do that. If atonement is simply a repayment of wrongdoing, I doubt there is a parent who has lost a child due to violence who would agree there is a repayment large enough, even the blood of the one who killed their child, that would satisfy them. All they really want is their child back.

If friendship with God is the goal of atonement, then a payment of blood by a third party, in this case Jesus, seems unlikely to accomplish that. If atonement is reconciliation or restored harmony between two parties, then how did this idea of blood sacrifice get attached to the meaning of the word? To help answer that, let's look at the origin of the word "atonement."

The word entered the English lexicon in the early 1500s, meaning "to be at one with another or be in harmony with another," or "at one with." This meaning is connected to the definition of reconciliation. In the 1520s, it became associated with Christian theology to mean reconciliation with God and roughly 100 years later to mean appeasement to an offended party, or in theology, to appease God for sin.[9]

Even though the word "atonement" didn't appear until the Middle Ages, people have been wrestling with the significance and meaning of Jesus's death since it happened over 2,000 years ago. If we look to scripture, we will find many different reasons for the death of Jesus. James Beilby and Paul R. Eddy, in their introduction to *The Nature of the Atonement: Four Views,* share ten reasons identified by John Driver for the death of Jesus in the New Testament. One reason is that there is a conflict between the forces of good and evil and we are susceptible to these forces. Therefore, Jesus came to die and rise again to achieve victory over the forces of evil, setting us free from those forces. Another reason is God's identification with the suffering of humanity through the cross. Still another is Jesus as our example to follow. Others are that Jesus was a martyr, a sacrifice, an appeaser of God's wrath, a ransom paid for sin, a bridge to God, one who makes us worthy before God, even a way to become part of God's forever family.[10] In chapter 2, we will explore in depth different theories of atonement but, as you can see, there are many different ways to understand the death of Jesus.

---

9. Harper, "Word Origin and History for Atonement," lines 1–4.
10. Beilby and Eddy, *The Nature of the Atonement,* 11.

If you want to consider only the writings of Paul, you will find six different ways he saw Jesus's death as bringing salvation. In Romans 5:12–19, Paul says that Jesus represents all humanity just as Adam represented all humanity. This means Jesus was our *representative* in death. In Romans 5:8–9, Paul says that Jesus was a blood *sacrifice* to save us from God's wrath. In Galatians 3:13, Paul says that Jesus became a curse for us to redeem us from the curse of the law. This means Jesus is our *redeemer* from a curse, which leads to death (Rom 8:2). In Galatians 2:20, Jesus died willingly because he *loved* us. Jesus saves us through love. In 2 Corinthians 5:18, Paul says Jesus reconciled us to God. Jesus is our *reconciler*. In Romans 3:25, Paul says that Jesus was a sacrifice of atonement. This generally is accepted to mean Jesus was our *substitute*.

Paul and all of the other New Testament writers have tried to make meaning out of the death of Jesus in many different ways. John Sanders, in *Atonement and Violence*, says the New Testament writers used a "host of ideas" to help those to whom they were writing grasp the reason for the death of Jesus within their own time and place.[11] With so many different ideas for the significance of Jesus's death, how do we make sense of it for ourselves? One way is to look at how lives are to be transformed through the salvation Jesus accomplished on the cross. Sanders believes the New Testament writers all agreed that the atonement was "intended to change lives individually and corporately."[12]

How Jesus's death changes lives is determined by the particular view of atonement you have. If you think Jesus died to set us free from the power of sin, then your life is changed because you now recognize that sin no longer needs to have power over you. If you believe Jesus died to take your place because God demanded your life as payment for sin, then your life is changed because you can live a life of gratitude for not having to face God's wrath for sin. If you believe Jesus died because God loves you, then your life is changed because God's love allows you to be more loving toward others, sharing that same love.

I like Sanders' approach that the New Testament writers all believed Jesus's death should have some effect on our lives. It suggests that while we can't all agree on the *meaning* of Jesus's death (redemptive,

---

11. Sanders, *Atonement and Violence*, xiii.
12. Sanders, *Atonement and Violence*, xi.

substitutionary, sacrificial, loving), we can agree on the *function* or purpose. I would suggest that the function is the heart of the gospel message, which Jesus came to proclaim. So what is the good news of Jesus's death? What I think personally, and what I propose here, is that there is no good news in the death of Jesus.

If the good news message is the one Jesus proclaimed, that God desires we be free of harsh spirits, free from oppression, be whole, and know dignity and the value of life, then the gospel is this: We are made friends of God by repenting, saying we are sorry for how we have oppressed others and devalued life—including our own and others'. And this seeking forgiveness is not just from God, but from those we have harmed. This asking of forgiveness is for individual sin and for sin committed corporately.

In Ezekiel 22:29–31, we find an interesting picture that speaks directly to the issue of seeking forgiveness for those we have wronged. It says:

> The people of the land have practiced extortion and committed robbery; they have oppressed the poor and needy, and have extorted from the alien without redress [making amends for wrongdoing]. And I sought for anyone among them who would repair the wall and stand in the breach before me on behalf of the land, so that I would not destroy it; but I found no one. Therefore I have poured out my indignation upon them; I have consumed them with the fire of my wrath; I have returned their conduct upon their heads, says the Lord God.

The people have committed sin by not maintaining equity or fairness. And they have not repaid the ones they have wronged. God looked for someone, anyone, who would repair this breach for the sake of the land, so that it would not be destroyed. There are a few important points in this text in relation to atonement. One, God is looking for someone to intercede on behalf of the people. This is what Moses did when God wanted to destroy the Israelites after bringing them out of Egypt (Exod 32:7–14), when they did not follow God's commands. God refers to them as stiff-necked and perverse, and wants to destroy them and start over with Moses.

But Moses intercedes on behalf of the people and reminds God of the promise to multiply the descendants of Abraham (verse 13). And God decides not to destroy the people. In a traditional view of atonement, this story of Moses works as a prefigure of Christ: God will destroy us for our sin, so Jesus intercedes on our behalf and God's mind is changed because of Jesus's willingness to stand in the gap. This analogy only goes so far, though. For one, Moses stops God with a reminder of God's own promise to Abraham. Could not Jesus, God's own Son, change God's mind also without requiring destruction and death? Secondly, it is the memory of God's friend Abraham that changes God's mind.

Paul also uses the Abraham-as-a-friend argument to support the inclusion of the Gentiles into the Abrahamic Promise. In Romans 4:16 and in Galatians 3:14, Paul says it is by sharing in the faith of Abraham that Gentiles are also included in the promise to Abraham, the promise that Abraham and his descendants would inherit the world. In Moses, the intercession comes so that the people will not be destroyed. In Ezekiel, the intercession comes so that the land would not be destroyed. In the New Testament period, it is so that the world will not be destroyed. But it is not blood sacrifice that stops God in all three instances. In the first two, it is God's friendship with one man, Abraham. In the third, the intercession is from God through God's own Son, Jesus. It is God living and breathing among us. It is God with us.

The second point in relation to the Ezekiel text is the reason for God's wrath. It is how the people treat one another. It is about how the people live in relationship with one another, whether or not they are loving toward one another. In *Transforming: The Bible & the Lives of Transgender Christians*, Austen Hartke notes that many transgender people experience minority stress, such as rejection, non-affirmation, victimization, and discrimination.[13] He concludes that these stressors, which are all relational, are "the effects of the fall manifesting in the

---

13. Hartke, *Transforming*, 38.

way human beings treat each other."[14] Perhaps a modern-day reading of Ezekiel would include the LGBTQ+ community and how many have been treated by the church. Would we take seriously how we treat one another, especially those we see as different from ourselves, if we tied our treatment of them to the wrath of God?

The writer of Hebrews has an interesting take on continuing in sin after one has come to the knowledge of the truth. First, if the truth is simply that Jesus died for your sins so that you can have eternal life, then your transaction with God has been completed and you are secure from God's wrath. But that's not what the writer of Hebrews says. In Hebrews 10:26–31, he says if after receiving the knowledge of the truth one continues to sin, there is no longer any sacrifice left and "it is a fearful thing to fall into the hands of the living God." This clearly indicates he did not believe in a "once saved, always saved" theology. If the sin that incurs the wrath of God is how we treat one another, then treating others with mercy, love, compassion, and empathy should be the center of our atonement theology.

Unfortunately, many of the atonement theories rely on an angry God who punishes for sin, where fear is the motivating factor, not love. For the famous "mini-gospel verse" of John 3:16—"For God so loved the world that he gave his only Son"—it is often assumed that Jesus was given as a blood offering for the sins of the world. But the actual Greek word used for "gave" in John 3:16 is the verb one uses when giving a gift. What if the gift God was giving was God in flesh, who came to heal and restore people unto God, not to be a bloody sacrifice? The angry God who punishes and the God of love who desires to heal are difficult to reconcile as the same God. One appears to look down on humanity waiting for us to mess up; the other looks down on humanity and says, "I am with you. In you I move and have my being. I forgive you." I recently had a spiritual experience that reinforced the latter.

I was visiting with a patient in his 80s in a rehabilitation center. He had suffered severe injuries in a car accident. As we visited, he shared his life's story with me. He was a lifelong Christian and dedicated member of his church. After he retired, his wife continued to work and

---

14. Hartke, *Transforming*, 38.

supported them through a successful business she owned. I mentioned that his wife must have really enjoyed her work to stick with it for so long. His reply was, "Oh, yes. Except for all the gays and blacks she had to deal with."

My eyes must have grown to be the size of saucers. Time seemed to slow down as my mind raced with how to respond to such a comment. While I have heard many times that when the elderly make racist and homophobic comments, it is because they are from a different generation, I still did not feel he could be excused! But then something happened inside me. The Holy Spirit moved and my heart was filled with overwhelming love for this man, in spite of his comment. And so I asked if I could pray with him. He said yes. And as I began to pray, he began to weep. I never addressed his sin; yet, it seemed the Holy Spirit was moving in him in ways that a rebuke from me could not have.

Julian of Norwich, the first English writer to be identified as a female, came to a similar conclusion about the nature of God. She fell seriously ill and, during her illness, on May 8, 1373, she had a series of visions she wrote about as the *Revelations of Divine Love*. In these visions, she saw Jesus and she felt the sin of the world. Then the feeling was quickly taken away and she heard Jesus say, "But all shall be well, all manner of things shall be well."[15] From this she concluded that God did not blame her for her sins and she "saw how Christ feels compassion for us because of sin."[16] God is a God of love and has compassion on us because of sin.

If we take the definition of atonement as it has been understood since the 1600s, that we owe God some sort of payment for sin, especially a payment in blood, how do we reconcile this with a God who seems to desire relationship, like the friendship shared with Abraham? In seminary, I had a preaching professor share that early in her career as a pastor, a man walked up to her after a church service and said, "Thanks for making me feel like a worm crawling toward the cross!" Indeed, if we are simply lost sinners with no hope, it is as though we are worms. I don't think you can build a healthy mutual relationship if one of the parties is seen as a worm.

---

15. Julian, *Revelations of Divine Love*, 22.
16. Julian, *Revelations of Divine Love*, 22.

In scripture, there are two primary ways in which the relationship between God and humanity is characterized. The first is the spousal relationship.[17] In Isaiah 54:5, we find, "For your Maker is your husband, the Lord of hosts is his name," and in Jeremiah 31:32, "It will not be like the covenant that I made with their ancestors when I took them by the hand to bring them out of the land of Egypt—a covenant that they broke, though I was their husband, says the Lord." In Hosea 2:16a, comes the promise that those who follow God will call God spouse: "On that day, says the Lord, you will call me, "My husband."

This is important to note because in all of these references, it is assumed that as a spouse, God is caring for Israel. In fact, in the rules for Christian living from Colossians 3:18–25, in verse 19 husbands are admonished to love their wives and never treat them harshly. Why would God then demand the harsh treatment of Jesus, and a blood sacrifice of Jesus, to cover the sin of humanity? If we are the spouse of God, we will never be treated harshly. One might present the argument that this only applies to those who have taken advantage of Christ's work on the cross. But the spousal references in the Old Testament would have been before the life of Jesus. In each appeal in the Old Testament, God desires the people to turn back to God as a loving spouse. There is no blood payment demanded for the return. It is always one of self-will.

The spousal relationship in the New Testament shifts to become one between Jesus and the church. But in the most well-known spousal reference between Jesus and his bride, it is not actually the church that is adorned like a bride to Christ, it is the New Jerusalem. And again, this is all about a caring relationship between God and humanity. The New Jerusalem is the dwelling place of God and humanity together as one. "See, the home of God is among mortals. He will dwell with them; they will be his peoples, and God himself will be with them" (Rev 21:3). This dwelling place with God is characterized as one where there is no more terror, no more tears, no more death. Life with God is one absent of violence and death.

The second primary relationship is that of the parent/child

17. I use spousal in this example because I in no way wish to imply that God is male. Also, with the use of spouse, I hope to be inclusive of all married relationships, not just those characterized by male and female. But please note, the scripture references all refer to God as male.

relationship as in Isaiah 43:6, ". . . bring my sons from far away and my daughters from the end of the earth," and Hosea 1:10, ". . . it shall be said to them, 'Children of the living God.'" In the New Testament, the parent/child relationship is described in Romans 8:16, "It is that very Spirit bearing witness with our spirit that we are children of God." And in Acts 17:28–29, while preaching in the marketplace in Athens, Paul says we are all the offspring or children of God. Just like in the spousal relationship, the parent relationship also shows God as the good and loving parent, not a harsh and demanding parent. In the Christian household rules in Colossians, parents are not to provoke their children or the children may lose heart. In other words, parents are to encourage their children (Col 3:21). God is our encourager.

There is no indication in scripture that parents are to exact payment from their children for wrongdoing, unless, of course, you want to include the scripture that allows parents to take disobedient children outside the city gates and stone them (Deut 21:18–21). Most scholars agree that this is for serious infractions that harm the community as a whole. Certainly, you could cite this verse as justification for God punishing humankind for sin. But as we have stated before, do you want to read the Bible through a lens of fear or one of love? For me personally, it was when I became a father that I began wrestling with the issue of atonement. I love my daughter. There is nothing she could do that would keep me from loving her or cause me to want to punish her with death. This is why I believe that the parent/child relationship is one of the most important examples to consider when discussing atonement.

As you think through your own position on atonement, I encourage you to sit with this position for a moment. How does it make you feel to think that Jesus did not have to die for your sin? Does it make you feel angry? Sad? Superior because you believe he did have to die to cover sin and you believe that is correct? Or do you feel a sense of relief? I want to speak to those of you who may be feeling defensive about this idea and ask you to answer the question, why?

Rob Bell, the author of many books on Christian theology, says in his book *Velvet Elvis: Repainting the Christian Faith* that we become defensive when we are challenged, especially with ideas that are in conflict with things we have held to be true for a long time. Essentially, we take the question of why Jesus died and come to the conclusion "for my sins" and use that belief to create a brick of knowledge. We take that brick and build a wall. As we figure out all the things we think Christianity is supposed to mean, we create more bricks and our wall gets bigger and more impenetrable. If someone challenges one of the ideas in our bricks, we have to defend it; otherwise, our wall might come crashing down.[18]

Defending our own views rarely changes the position of another. In *Talking Across the Divide,* Justin Lee points out that it can be frustrating when we truly feel that we are correct and other people, groups, or organizations believe the opposite of what we do and are just as entrenched in their feeling of being correct. The feeling becomes one of why bother talking if no one is going to change their mind?[19] But changing someone's mind, while certainly a goal, shouldn't be the endgame. The result we need to be working toward is listening to one another in order to create dialogue. Lee says it is counterintuitive, but true, that dialogue actually creates more change than debate.[20]

As we move into chapter 2, it is my hope we can create a dialogue surrounding our own views of atonement without debate. Let me say now that it is not my goal to convince you of anything. My hope is that you will carefully consider the issue and how it impacts your own relationship with God.

---

18. Bell, *Velvet Elvis,* 26.
19. Lee, *Talking Across the Divide,* 28.
20. Lee, *Talking Across the Divide,* 31.

Chapter 2
What Are the Different Theories of Atonement?

You do well if you really fulfill the royal law
according to the scripture, "You shall love your neighbor as yourself."
—*James 2:8*

If you have not seen the YouTube video of sociologist Brené Brown's sermon at the Washington National Cathedral on January 21, 2018, I recommend you do a search on YouTube and watch it. In her sermon, she says her spirituality and faith in God is about all human beings being connected, and because it is God who connects all human beings, that connection cannot be severed. We can forget the connection, but that doesn't mean it doesn't exist. She concludes with the phrase, "Be you. Be here. Belong."[1] The sense of belonging, the idea that we all belong to God and each other, is reflected in Jesus's words, "'You shall love the Lord your God with all your heart, and with all your soul, and with all your mind.' This is the greatest and first commandment. And a second is like it: 'You shall love your neighbor as yourself'" (Matt 22:37–38). The apostle Paul made this the core of his teaching and ethic for life.

In Galatians 5:14, Paul says, "For the whole law is summed up in a single commandment, 'You shall love your neighbor as yourself.'" Paul wrote some of the most beautiful words about love in scripture. I Corinthians 13, known as the Love Chapter, is read at almost every wedding. Paul declares in verse 7 that love bears all things and never ends. In Romans 12:9–21, Paul lays out how we as Christians are to live in love. We are to be genuine in our love and even outdo one another in showing honor. We are to love and bless our enemies. We are to overcome evil with good. Many of the theories of atonement are rooted in the writings of Paul. So as we look now at the different theories, I offer

---

1. Brown, "January 21, 2018: (HD) Sunday Sermon," YouTube.

thoughts after each one through the lens of love.

I also encourage you as you read to offer yourself love, especially if you feel tension regarding viewpoints that make you uncomfortable or with which you disagree. Be in dialogue with yourself and ask the questions: Why do I believe a certain viewpoint over others? Why do I feel tension regarding theories with which I am uncomfortable? Can I explore different viewpoints of faith, trusting that God is with me and that it is okay? Please ask yourself these questions as we go through the following theories of atonement. There are many. Some of these theories have been around for centuries; some are relatively new. And there are theories not covered here. One of the joys of the Christian life is the gift of love for God, others, and self that Jesus shared and Paul affirmed. Use that gift to explore the ideas that others have put forth to answer the question, what is the significance of Jesus's death?

Before we launch into each theory, I feel it is important to restate my position that atonement as a repayment for wrongdoing is not necessary for the Christian faith and for God to love us and for us to be in relationship with God. In his book *Saved from Sacrifice: A Theology of the Cross,* S. Mark Heim notes that critics of atonement theology are often critics because they see no redemptive example in Jesus's death.[2] I am such a critic. I see no redemptive value in Jesus's death. Heim sums up what I am trying to say perfectly: "Critics do not find here any meaningful explanation of why that death would help. It is an 'empty' death, and seems to invite or require the postulation of some hidden divine transaction to give it [the death of Jesus] the meaning it lacks on the face of things."[3] If we go back to the idea that what God desired all along is to be in relationship with humanity, then Jesus's death would indeed be empty because death ends relationships, it does not start them.

I want us to be comfortable with the notion that Jesus's death may have just been the result of humanity's bent toward violence. Because of this, God knew the sending of Jesus would result in his death. Look at the parable of the tenants in Matthew 21:28–46, Mark 12:1–12, and Luke 20:9–19. In this parable, the vineyard is leased out to tenants and

---

2. Heim, *Saved from Sacrifice,* 296.
3. Heim, *Saved from Sacrifice,* 297.

the owner sends his servants to collect his portion of the earnings at the end of each harvest. But the tenants refuse to pay. They resort to violence, beating up the servants and killing some. So the owner sends his son believing that they will listen to him. But they recognize that the son is the heir to the vineyard, so they kill him too. This parable is clearly about Jesus. He is the trusted son sent by God to God's people. The parable is not meant to be a mystery. The meaning is to be clear, that Jesus is going to die.

The foreknowledge of God that Jesus would be killed and Jesus's willingness to come do not prove that God wanted or needed Jesus to die. Psalm 11:6 says that God's soul hates the lover of violence. The Hebrew word for "soul" in this verse means *vitality* or *breath*. Literally, that which gives life. God, who gives all life, is opposed to violence. So how do we reconcile this image of God who abhors violence with the God who destroys the world with a flood, saving only Noah and his family? As discussed in chapter 1, we have to live with the fact that our sacred texts endorse and condone the very things that they also oppose. And this is not always comfortable. So consider Psalm 18:25–26:

> With the loyal you show yourself loyal;
> with the blameless you show yourself blameless;
> with the pure you show yourself pure;
> and with the crooked you show yourself perverse.

How we see God may have to do with what's in our own hearts. This actually bears witness to what Jesus taught when he said, "For out of the abundance of the heart the mouth speaks. The good person brings good things out of a good treasure, and the evil person brings evil things out of an evil treasure" (Matt 12:34b–35). This is true not only for how we read and interpret scripture, but also for the writers of scripture. That means the writers of scripture had an image of God in mind when they wrote. That image was influenced by their own hearts as well as the time period and culture in which they lived. The same is true for those who have gone before us in the Christian faith. As they interpreted scripture in order to understand why Jesus died, they used their own understandings of God, influenced by their own time period and culture, to come up with the theories below.

I also am doing the same thing that the biblical authors and church fathers did. I am choosing to see God, the life and death and resurrection of Jesus, and the continuing work of the Holy Spirit through an interpretive lens of love. This will be the lens through which I offer some thoughts following each atonement theory below.

Recapitulation Theory – One of the earliest views of atonement was first presented in the second century by Irenaeus, a bishop of France who was born in Smyrna, in what is now Turkey. He was raised in a Christian home, so he did not convert. In his theory, Jesus is the second Adam. Jesus accomplished what Adam could not, which is obedience to God. Jesus's obedience overturned or corrected Adam's disobedience, thereby releasing humanity from Adam's error and restoring relationship with God. In this theory, death came into the world because of Adam, so by undoing what Adam did, Jesus destroys death. Recapitulation means a restatement of an original point, or a return to an original position. Jesus's death and resurrection returned humanity to its original connection to God.

Thoughts: Irenaeus's position is well thought out. It makes sense that if death entered the world through one man as Paul indicates in 1 Corinthians 15:21–22, then death would be overcome by Jesus, the God-man. The theory also is consistent in that it views sin as disobedience, and Jesus corrected or saved us from this sin by being obedient where Adam was not. In this theory, death is necessary because it was the result of sin and Jesus had to die to be resurrected and overcome death.

This is substitutionary atonement. In order for us to return to God's plan of harmony with humanity, a substitute is needed. God cannot forgive our disobedience or overcome death without a substitute. If we go back to chapter 1 where I defined sin as not living in love as God created us to, resulting in broken relationship between us and God and each other, then the disobedience of Adam was a loveless act. He showed a lack of love for God and himself by acting selfishly. Surely all that would be required, instead of a substitutionary death, is recognition of wrongdoing and repentance, an asking for forgiveness. Requiring a substitute to seek our forgiveness for us is not true repentance. True repentance is when we are pained by our hurtful or sinful actions and seek reconciliation with the one we have offended.

One additional consideration regarding Irenaeus's theory, which will also hold true for many of the other theories, is that it presumes that Jesus completed a divine act to reconnect us to God, an act that we as humans could not achieve on our own. This assumes an exclusive right by Christians to have access to God. It is what is called *supersessionism,* which is the belief that the church superseded Israel as God's chosen people. It implies an exclusionary approach to God that only believers in Jesus can have restored relationship with God. But if we look at this presumption through a lens of love, we have to ask questions: What happens to those who are also created in God's good image, also subject to the fall, but have never heard of Jesus? Or what if they hear of Jesus, but have no desire to accept Jesus as their substitute?

If Jesus came to point us all to the God who loves us, and there is no need for a substitute between us and God, then Christianity does not need to be exclusionary. It can lovingly relate to all people, regardless of whether or not they believe the same things. This means that all who point people to God are doing the work of Jesus. It is not an exclusionary work for Jesus or his followers alone. In Luke 9:50, Jesus said those who do his work of healing and restoration, regardless of whether they believe the same thing, should not be stopped, "for whoever is not against you is for you."

Ransom Theory – Another early view of atonement, the Ransom Theory, is credited to Origen, an early church father who lived in the third century. His theory states that Adam and Eve gave over their rights to Satan in the Garden of Eden when they ate of the fruit. This meant that God must pay the devil a ransom to win back humanity from the devil's clutches. But when the devil accepted Jesus's death as payment for the ransom, he did not realize that death could not hold Jesus, thereby winning all humanity back from the devil. Some found it difficult to accept this theory as they could not reconcile an all-powerful

God owing something to the devil, so others adopted the theory with the change that humanity ransomed itself to sin and death. Jesus as a ransom set humanity free from sin and death.

Thoughts: Origen's theory also holds up well if one considers together the actions of the snake, an image for the devil, in the Garden of Eden and Jesus's wrestling with Satan in the wilderness for forty days. While in the wilderness, Satan offers Jesus food, authority over the kingdoms of the world, and the opportunity to test God and Jesus's own sonship, all of which Jesus refuses. Satan offering Jesus these things, particularly authority over the world powers, indicates that Satan has some autonomy over these. The original plan was for humanity to have power to create the kingdoms of the world, but they are now in Satan's hands, given away by Adam and Eve.

With all the poverty, health issues, and broken government systems in the world, it is easy to see that there appears to be an evil influence. But as in the Garden of Eden, humanity has a choice of whether or not to cooperate with those evil influences. In Genesis, when Cain is angry with Abel, God warns Cain that he must get his anger under control for there is evil lurking at his door, whose desire is for him. This personification of evil is notable, but this is after Adam and Eve have supposedly ransomed away humanity's rights. God tells Cain he must master the evil at his door. God does not indicate that Cain is bound in some way to the devil. Cain still maintains the ability to choose evil or good. This indicates that no ransom is necessary. If the point is that humankind cannot ultimately choose good because of the ransom to the devil, sin, and death, then God is not being genuine to Cain, knowing that Cain has no power to choose good.

In most of the atonement theories, God is considered genuine, honorable, and just. But if God offers a choice to Cain, knowing that Cain cannot choose a better path, then God appears to be unjust, or at the very least, not honorable. If we assume that Satan had no power over humanity until they chose the fruit, and Jesus's death was necessary as payment to take that power away from Satan, then why did Jesus's death and resurrection not end evil in the world? In traditional substitutionary atonement theology, the answer to this question is that while Jesus won the victory, every human must choose Jesus as their substitute or ransom before the enemy, Satan, can be bound once and for all.

This presents a problem in that once someone becomes a Christian, they do not stop sinning. Evil still seems to hold sway. In Paul's ethic of love, we are called to forgive those who harm us, to keep no record of wrongs. This indicates we continue to have choice. It also presents a sticky argument in terms of the character of God. It is generally accepted that God is love as noted in I John 4. If God is love, then Paul's description of love would also describe God. If this is true then God as love would keep no record of wrongs. Our wrongdoing is forgotten by God because that is God's very nature. God does not need a substitute or a payment nor owe a payment to any other entity. God can do whatever God wants to do, and if that action is consistent with love, then it is one of forgiveness without repayment.

Satisfaction Theory – The Ransom Theory was the dominant view for much of the early church. But in the twelfth century, Anselm, an archbishop of Canterbury, felt that God should not owe anyone anything, especially the devil. And if anyone owed God anything, it was humanity. So he developed the Satisfaction Theory. This theory states that because God is a God of justice, God's justice must be honored, so humanity must pay a debt to God to satisfy God's honor. Jesus, by coming to earth and dying, satisfied God's honor.

Thoughts: Anselm's theory does not hold up as well as the first two theories. The first two are at least rooted in the biblical narrative. Anselm's theory relies more heavily on judicial thinking. And it is most clearly substitutional in nature. Jesus is our substitute to satisfy God's honor.

Anselm clearly is taking into consideration God's nature in this view. God is a God of honor. But while it definitely is trying to make sense of Jesus's death, the theory does not take Jesus's message into consideration. Jesus's message was to free captives from oppression, to heal, and to restore relationships. You could actually say that Jesus's very life was God's message. In Jesus, God is saying, "I am with you." In Anselm's theory, God is set apart from humanity as a judge looking down.

Lastly, as noted above, if love keeps no record of wrongs, and we as imitators of Christ are to live out this ethic of love by not keeping a record of wrongs, why is God asking us to do something God is not willing to do? We are to forgive those who have wronged us, but God cannot forgive without a repayment? It seems that if it is God's honor that needs to be satisfied as Anselm indicates, then God would not require something of us that God would not also do.

Moral Influence Theory – In response to Anselm's Satisfaction Theory, Peter Abelard, a twelfth-century theologian and thinker, agreed that the Ransom Theory was a poor one because God should not owe the devil anything. But he also did not agree with Anselm. Abelard did not see God as harsh, judgmental, and needing to be satisfied with the repayment of a debt of honor. He saw God as loving and wanted other people to see God this way too. He also felt that because God loved us, God did not hold our sin against us.[4] So Abelard proposed the Moral Influence Theory or Example Theory that Jesus came as an example to humanity of God's love. Jesus's death should inspire us to be better people by loving God and neighbor.

Thoughts: I like Abelard's position of seeing God as loving and not harsh. This theory is not substitutionary as the other models. Instead of Jesus being a substitute, he is our example. It makes all of Jesus's life, death, and resurrection important. What is interesting is that this theory is not about atonement. If we use the definition of atonement as a repayment for wrongdoing, the Moral Influence Theory does not work. In this theory, Jesus's death is an example of what a self-sacrificial life to God looks like. This theory relies heavily on Philippians 2:1–8 where Jesus empties himself, becoming the least, even to the point of death. If the original definition of atonement is used, which says that atonement is about becoming one or living in harmony, then this theory works. But the Moral Influence Theory still does not show why Jesus had to die.

To be a positive moral example that inspires others, death is not necessary. A positive moral example is all about how someone lives

---

4. Sanders, *Atonement and Violence,* xiv. Abelard's position echoes the vision Julian of Norwich had in which Christ tells her, "God has compassion on humanity because of sin."

their life. Jesus could have at the end of his ministry commissioned the disciples and ascended to God as he did in Matthew 28 without dying. The Moral Influence Theory does not answer the question, why did Jesus have to die?

Penal Substitutionary Theory – In the sixteenth century, those who wanted to see reform happen in the Catholic Church, such as Martin Luther and John Calvin, began the Protestant Reformation. Along with the departure from the Catholic Church came a departure from the Recapitulation Theory, the Ransom Theory, and the Satisfaction Theory. Uniquely Protestant, the Penal Substitutionary Theory says that God's justice demands a sacrifice for sin. This is different from the Satisfaction Theory, which says that God's honor was offended and that honor must be repaid. The Penal Substitutionary Theory says that God's holiness and justice demands a punishment for sin. Instead of honor being repaid, a punishment must be made. So Jesus took the punishment God demanded for sin.

Thoughts: This theory is problematic in the same way the other substitutionary models are. Any substitute model removes the individual from directly seeking forgiveness for the wrong committed. As with Abelard's objection to the Satisfaction Theory, this theory also characterizes God as harsh with the addition of a demand for punishment due to sin. If we go back to Adam and Eve in the Garden of Eden, where sin is to have originated, God's response was one of love by providing skins to cover their nakedness, a nakedness that neither they nor God had any issue with prior to their eyes being opened to both evil and good. Even their need to leave the garden was an act of love by God, for God says it was for their own protection: "See, the man has become like one of us, knowing good and evil; and now, he might reach out his hand and take also from the tree of life, and eat, and live forever" (Gen 3:22).

In looking at our world today, and our historical background of violence, it is not difficult to see the danger of living forever in a perpetual cycle of never-ending violence, from which even death cannot release you. From this perspective, death is a gift, not a punishment. The hope that we hold as Christians is that when God does end death, the threat of pain and violence also will end (Rev 21:3–4).

Governmental Theory – In the seventeenth century, Hugo Grotius, a Dutch legal expert, published many works on the law, but his most popular work was *The Truth of the Christian Religion.*[5] Using his legal background to frame his understanding of God, Grotius saw God as the great moral governor of the cosmos. As such, God is the rightful judge of that which is wrong; therefore, God alone can punish for sin. Building off of Grotius's work, theologians developed the Governmental Theory, stating that Jesus was a substitute for the punishment that sin deserves, but not as an exact payment for sin as in the Penal Substitutionary Theory. In the Governmental model, Jesus appeased God's displeasure with sin.

Thoughts: This is an improvement over the Penal Substitutionary Theory in that it reflects the harm sin causes both God and humanity, but it still characterizes God as a judge needing to be satisfied. This theory depicts God as a removed agent, not actively involved in people's real lives, waiting only to judge behavior. But the preferred way the prophets described God in the Old Testament is as a loving parent or spouse, actively engaged in people's lives. When God did act as judge in the Old Testament, it was overwhelmingly because of idolatry. Worshipping other gods was sin in that it broke relationship with the one true God. Love is about relationship, not punishment.

Christus Victor Theory – In 1931, Gustaf Aulén, a Lutheran bishop in the Church of Sweden, wrote a book called *Christus Victor.* In it, he took the Ransom Theory's premise that humanity was enslaved to sin, death, and the devil or evil, but eliminated the need for payment to the devil or God. Christ's death instead set humanity free from its bondage to sin, death, and evil. Aulén believed that this was truly the view of the church throughout its history, calling it the "classic" view.[6] John Sanders summarizes the Christus Victor Theory:

The powers of evil work through individual humans as

---

5. Onuma, "Hugo Grotius," para. 5.
6. Thompson, "Christus Victor," para. 6.

well as political and economic social structures to get humans to treat one another in ways contrary to how God would have us live, thus resulting in sin and death. Consequently, humans have become enslaved to these powers and cannot liberate themselves. Jesus, however, by faithfully following the will of God did not become enslaved to the powers of evil. In his battle against evil Jesus is killed and it seems the forces of evil have won. Through his resurrection, however, Jesus triumphed over the evil powers and works to liberate humans from their enslavement. Thus the resurrection is key to our salvation.[7]

Thoughts: This theory is noteworthy in that it makes Jesus's life, death, and resurrection important, not just his death. It also provides for the ongoing salvation of humanity and the continued work of Christ. It, like the Moral Influence Theory, is not substitutionary. Jesus's death is the result of a battle between good and evil. This cosmic or spiritual battle is covered in scriptures like Ephesians 6:12 and Colossians 2:15.

While the most comprehensive in giving meaning to Jesus's life, death, and resurrection, this theory is like all the others in relying on particular scriptures, particularly those concerning spiritual warfare. This is problematic in that the New Testament characterizes God's kingdom as "righteousness and peace and joy in the Holy Spirit" (Rom 14:17). James, the leader of the first church in Jerusalem and the half-brother of Jesus, says there are two kinds of wisdom—one that is earthly, unspiritual, and devilish, leading to envy, selfishness, and disorder, and the other "from above," pure, peaceable, gentle, willing to yield, and full of mercy (Jas 3:13–18). God's kingdom is peaceful and gentle. If we consider Jesus's use of nonviolence and his unwillingness to use violence to keep himself from dying as a spiritual weapon, then the Christus Victor Theory of spiritual warfare works as a theory that nonviolence defeats the evil powers.[8]

Nonviolence as a way to defeat evil can be supported through

---

7. Sanders, *Atonement and Violence*, xiii.
8. Jesus declares in Matthew 26:53 that he could call down angels to protect him and the disciples, but he chooses not to.

the lens of love. So is there any concern with this theory? The main concern with the Christus Victor Theory is that it locates evil outside of us. In other words, evil influences us and while we have power over it at times and not at other times, our responsibility for our sin lies only in our ability to resist it. What then of the political and economic systems Jesus defeated in Christus Victor? If we grew up white in South Africa during apartheid and not knowing any better contributed to the oppression of blacks, at what point is that "our sin"? In Christus Victor, sin, death, and evil are cosmic forces enslaving us. Since we both knowingly and unknowingly participate with these forces even after confessing lordship of Christ, this creates a limited atonement or "not yet" change.

In Romans 6:5–14, Paul indicates that Christ's release of us from our enslavement to sin means that we have the power to not sin. In verse 14 he says, "For sin will have no dominion over you, since you are not under law but under grace." Since we know we still sin and participate in the political and economic systems of sin, some of which we have no control over, the Christus Victor Theory offers a limited atonement not to be fully realized until the return of Christ and the New Jerusalem. But then why did Jesus die? If things remain the same until Jesus returns, why die at all? God will still accomplish God's plan of love to remove all sin, death, and evil at the end. If Jesus's conquering of these powers is a foretaste of what is to come, then it is not atoning at all. It is not repayment for wrongdoing nor is it achieving harmony with God and humanity.

Accident Theory – In the early twentieth century, Albert Schweitzer, famous for his humanitarian efforts as a doctor in the jungles of Africa, also wrote about his understanding of Jesus Christ. Schweitzer believed that Jesus did not realize he was the Messiah until after his baptism. After his baptism, Jesus began preaching the kingdom of God and believed himself to be the one to usher it into existence. This put Jesus at odds with the political and religious leaders of his day, which led to his execution. Schweitzer believed Jesus did not expect to be executed and that his death was an accident; therefore, his death was not atoning.

Thoughts: Like the Moral Influence Theory and the Scapegoat

Theory to follow, the Accident Theory is not a substitutionary atonement model because Jesus is not a substitute for humanity. In fact, Jesus's death has little or no significant meaning other than that he was a revolutionary. Aside from Schweitzer's own belief, the theory could be used to conclude that Jesus's death did unite his followers and create a religion of love that works to end systematic violence and bring peace. In this instance, the Accident Theory is atoning in terms of the first definition of atonement, that which creates harmony.

Still, Jesus's death would not be necessary for God to accomplish this unity. In Acts 17, when Paul is at the Areopagus, he tells the Athenians that God is not served by human hands nor does God live in shrines made by humans. Nor does God need anything from mortals since God gives life and breath to every living thing. Instead, it was as the poets of Athens said, "we live and move and have our being" in God (Acts 17:28). If God gives life to every living thing and needs nothing from humans, then any theory of atonement is a waste of time. There is nothing we can provide to God that would offer repayment or unify creation.

If unity through the harmony of all things, a true "at-one-ment," is the goal and there is nothing humanity can do for God, then only God can bring about true harmony. Our only action is to cooperate with God in accomplishing this unity. Death does not bring unity, only separation. But as revealed in the resurrection, death is never the end precisely because only God can give life. Death cannot forever separate or end. In death, even as a seed falls to the ground, it springs up bringing new life. In this example, death is not accidental but part of God's renewing cycle of life.

Through the lens of love, the Accident Theory offers help in understanding the death of Jesus only in that those who stand up to power and authority for the sake of love, as Jesus did, will most likely lose their life. And, honestly, this is not accidental. It is premeditated murder by those who wish to silence the voice of good. The death of one who is working to end violence and bring about God's kingdom of love is a loss for the world, not a gain. Jesus's death, even if accidental as Schweitzer suggests, is a loss.

Scapegoat Theory – In the mid-twentieth century, a man named René Girard, who is best known for writing and teaching literature and philosophy, became interested in human nature. For the early part of his life he was an agnostic, but in reading the great literature of his day he converted to Christianity and became a practicing Roman Catholic.[9] As part of his research, Girard developed what he called mimetic theory, which is the idea that humans learn and adapt through imitation.[10] This led him to develop the Scapegoat Theory of atonement. This theory says that humans learn from a very early age that violence is a way of life.

For Girard, God opposes violence in all its forms; therefore, Jesus came to be a scapegoat or victim of violence to expose our human leaning toward violence and to bear witness to all victims of violence. Jesus then saves humanity by our willingness to accept our violent tendencies and, once recognized, we can turn from them to truly achieve the peace that surpasses all understanding, which God intended us to have.

Thoughts: The Scapegoat Theory is not a substitutionary atonement theory. In Girard's position, Jesus did not come as a substitute for humanity, but as a witness to the human desire for sin, in this case violence. It is closest to the Moral Influence Theory as neither is technically an atonement theory based on the definition of atonement as a repayment for wrongdoing. If we follow the original definition of atonement as living in harmony, then this theory works because Jesus came to point us to God's way of perfect peace and harmony. It also provides a reason for Jesus's death in that God came to identify with victims and reveal to us our desire to imitate death.

I confess I like Girard's theory very much. In the Christus Victor Theory, evil is located outside of us. In the Scapegoat Theory, evil is part of our nature, and we participate in both good and evil. This rings true, especially if we use Sanders's definition from *Atonement and Violence* where violence is defined as "any use of force or coercion that involves some kind of hurt or injury—whether this coercion be physical or nonphysical, personal or institutional, incidental or structural."[11]

---

9. Andrade, "René Girard," para. 6.
10. Andrade, "René Girard," para. 8–9.
11. Sanders, *Atonement and Violence*, xii.

Sanders goes on to say, "Clearly this includes harm or damage done to another such as killing or war, but it also includes such things as economic oppression and racism."[12] All of us have participated in some form of oppression, whether knowingly or unknowingly, including thoughts or words of anger. In Matthew 5:21–22, Jesus said if you call someone an empty-headed fool, you are guilty of murder. Jesus took the issue of actions and related them to the human heart, which is where human action begins. Even if we think it, it's like we have done it. This seems to complement the Scapegoat Theory.

Now let's look at the Scapegoat Theory through the lens of love. Much as in the Moral Influence Theory, Jesus's life reveals to us God's desire to identify with victims and for us to turn from our violent ways. Being created in the good image of God, an image of love, we innately have the capacity of Jesus for empathetic compassion, not just the drive toward anger and violence. According to the documentary *I Am* by Tom Shadyac, human beings are prewired to help and care for one another, to share resources, to feel one another's pain for the purpose of human survival.[13]

In the film, he debunks the notion that humans are created for survival of the fittest. In fact, he says it is the opposite. In Girard's theory, humans imitate violence and have no choice until they recognize this tendency in the death of Jesus. But according to the science presented by Shadyac, we are innately wired to imitate goodness and compassion first and foremost. Two opposing views, one based on social science, the other on brain science. Which is it?

The reality is Jesus did not need to die or become a scapegoat in order for humanity to recognize that violence is damaging. It is Jesus's life that witnessed to the power of God's good to transform. Walter Wink, a biblical scholar who was shaped by his work in the American civil rights movement and his work in South Africa to end apartheid, likes to highlight Romans 12:1 when he talks about the violence of the scapegoat sacrificial system. Romans 12:1 says that we are to "present our bodies as a living sacrifice" (emphasis Wink's).[14] It is in living like Jesus that change is brought to the world.

---

12. Sanders, *Atonement and Violence*, xii.
13. Shadyac, *I Am*, DVD.
14. Wink, *The Powers That Be*, 95.

Kaleidoscopic Theory – As time has progressed, more and more people are asking questions about the significance of Jesus's death, resulting in more and more theories being offered. I have included this modern view, the Kaleidoscopic Theory of atonement, because it is unique in that it tries to make sense of all the different theories that can be supported by scripture. Joel B. Green, a professor of New Testament at Asbury Theological Seminary, believes Jesus is the "interpretive matrix for understanding the pattern of God's story, the lens through which to read our story within the story of God."[15] In this view, Jesus is sacrificial lamb, Jesus ratifies the new covenant between God and humanity, Jesus is the substitute offering for human sin, Jesus is to enamor humanity so fully that they enter into the narrative of scripture and are transformed by his sacrifice, "embody[ing] his life as their own."[16] Essentially, Green states that different theories of atonement are more attractive to some than to others and appeal differently to different people across time; therefore, "an expansive range of images and models for comprehending and articulating the atonement" is necessary.[17]

Thoughts: I included the Kaleidoscopic view precisely because there are so many different ways to support different views of the atonement through scripture. It lets us incorporate them all. One particular view may ultimately draw someone to God, while another draws someone else. In Acts 17:26–27, Paul states that God's desire is that all people recognize their connection to God, and Paul is willing to incorporate the Athenian poets as well as a statue to an unknown god as ways of drawing people to God. Green's view makes sense.

The approach to choosing an atonement theory that works for you is fine as long as it is realized that the view chosen is not the only theory that works or has validity. This would include the theory I propose, which is that no atonement theories are necessary. To support multiple theories to appeal to as many people as possible means one must also support that no theories are necessary either. I would also caution that some theories can be harmful. So while a particular theory may work for one person, it may be damaging to another. We will look

---

15. Green, "Kaleidoscopic View," 182.
16. Green, "Kaleidoscopic View," 175–78.
17. Green, "Kaleidoscopic View," 185.

at some of the damage that substitutionary atonement theories have caused individuals in chapter 8.

Chapter 3
Is Atonement Necessary?

Jesus came to Galilee, proclaiming the good news of God,
and saying, "The time is fulfilled, and the kingdom of God has come near;
repent, and believe in the good news."
—Mark 1:14b–15

So what is the good news message if it is not "Jesus died for my sins?" This is one of the most difficult issues to overcome as our brains create new ways of seeing and believing. John Sanders, a professor of religious studies at Hendrix College in Arkansas, enjoys asking his students to explain the gospel to him as though he is not a Christian and interested in learning more about Christianity. The narrative students typically share is that we are all sinners and therefore guilty before a just and holy God. So God sent Jesus to die for us so that our sins may be forgiven. This is the dominant view in America and it is a substitutionary model. Sanders then asks the students clarifying questions like, "What you are saying is that if I place my trust in the work of Jesus then I am completely forgiven and do not have to follow Jesus after that?"[1]

There are two things Sanders is attempting to get his students to realize. One, in substitutionary atonement models, which the majority of the theories are, a transaction between God and humans is taking place. Once that transaction is complete, both parties have fulfilled their obligation so there is no longer any further action required. If there is further action required, then the gospel is no longer a simple transaction of accepting Jesus's death as an atoning and substitute sacrifice for sin. Two, while Christians have agreed from the beginning of Christianity that Jesus is the savior, they have not always agreed on how Jesus saves. Sanders says, "The New Testament writers used a wide array of images and conceptual metaphors to convey the gospel message . . . in order to

---

1. Sanders, *Atonement and Violence*, ix.

articulate the meaning of the atonement in ways that would resonate with the cultural ethos of the day."[2]

In other words, different atonement theories developed over time as people tried to explain why Jesus died and how his life, death, and resurrection still related to their own daily lives, in their own lifetime, and in their time period. We are still doing that today. As more and more Christians are deconstructing their faith—that is, questioning the things they were taught and grew up believing about Christianity—the idea that God required a blood sacrifice for sin, especially the life of God's own son, has become difficult to reconcile with a God who is supposed to be perfect love, as declared in I John 4:8 and 4:16. Does perfect love require violence?

In his book *Atonement and Violence,* Sanders quotes from an article in the evangelical magazine *Christianity Today* titled "The Gospel of Jesus Christ: An Evangelical Celebration." The article's author asserts that there is no gospel without penal substitutionary atonement.[3] For many Christians, the idea that Jesus had to die for our sins has become synonymous with the gospel. Yet, God requiring an act of violence or allowing the killing of Jesus to accomplish a greater good goes against the witness of Jesus as to what God requires. In Mark 3:4–5, Jesus is angry because the religious leaders will not answer a simple question that saving life is greater than killing. I believe it is time, as more and more Christians are rethinking Jesus as our substitute for sin, to reexamine what the gospel is, how it addresses sin, and what it means for salvation.

Gospel means good news. The good news of Jesus Christ is simply this: God loves us. Love does not require punishment and death. In fact, God is not the God of death, but of life. In Matthew 22:23–33, the Sadducees who did not believe those who had died would be given new life by God at the resurrection, question Jesus about this by telling him a story about a woman whose husband died before they had any children. As was the custom, she was to marry another brother to keep the family name going on behalf of the brother who had died. According to the story, there were seven brothers and they all married her and died without her having any children. The question to Jesus is, "Whose wife

2. Sanders, *Atonement and Violence,* ix.
3. Sanders, *Atonement and Violence,* xv.

will she be in the resurrection?"

Jesus's response is that the Sadducees are mistaken. Life after death is different than life here on earth. Then he corrects their understanding of scripture by saying, "Have you not read what was said to you by God, 'I am the God of Abraham, the God of Isaac, and the God of Jacob'? He is God not of the dead, but of the living" (verses 31–32). This can be looked at in two ways. Was Jesus saying Abraham, Isaac, and Jacob, though long dead on earth, are alive with God now? Or was he saying, do not worry about what happens after you die, concentrate on how you are living your life now?

Is it possible it could have both meanings? Regardless, it is significant in defining what the gospel means in light of the atonement. God is not the God of death. God is life! Just as the Sadducees were focused on the wrong thing, we are focused on the wrong thing in substitutionary atonement. We are focused on death, not life. And the life God gives us is not just physical life like eating, breathing, sleeping, and moving about, but how we live life in relationship with others. Life is about love. As I stated earlier, the idea that God requires violence in order to bring life became crazy to me when I became a parent.

I love my daughter more than I ever thought it was possible. The idea of committing violence against her as punishment for wrongdoing does not even register in my brain. When I was growing up, spanking as punishment for doing something wrong was very common. I learned early on in parenting that it is easy to fall back on the way you were parented. But I will never forget the first time I spanked my daughter. She had been told to leave the living room window blinds alone. But she would not stay away from them. And sure enough, she ended up pulling them down. My initial reaction was, "You were told to leave the blinds alone. And you didn't, so now I'm going to spank you." I swatted her bottom with my hand and the look on her face tore my heart in two. It was a look of shock, betrayal, and hurt.

Even though I had learned in parenting class before she was born that we cannot teach our children not to hit if we spank them, I still spanked her. After it happened, I regretted it immediately. But the remorse made me realize something important. Spanking was a punishment. And while it may make her think twice before she does something she has been asked not to do, it damaged my relationship with her. That was apparent by the look on her face. My job as a parent is to protect and nurture her, to guide her, to help her make good and positive choices. Violence was not the way to do that. Violence would only produce fear and resentment, not love.

In Matthew 7:9–11, Jesus asks the question, "If your child asks for bread, will you give him a stone? Or if he asks for a fish, will you give him a snake?" The obvious answer is "No." Jesus continues, "If you then, who are evil, know how to give good gifts to your children, how much more will your Father in heaven give good things to those who ask him!" We love our children. We give them the things they need like food, shelter, clothing, even toys and a whole lot more when it comes to opportunities like extracurricular activities at school, sports camps, gymnastics, ballet, soccer, football, art classes, and on and on. If we who are sinful do these things for our children, our children who talk back to us, who oftentimes don't seem to appreciate the sacrifices made for them, how much more good will God do for us as God's children?

This is why I think we've gotten the whole idea of atonement wrong. We are the work of God's hands. We are God's children. Yes, we've made mistakes. We have sinned against God, ourselves, and others. But does God demand we or Jesus pay for those mistakes? God is a far better parent than we could ever be. And much more loving, too. When Jesus was on the cross, he did not say, "Father, thank you for allowing me to make a way for your wayward children to come back to you." No, Jesus said, "Father, forgive them for they know not what they do."

Is killing the one who had healed sickness and disease, miraculously provided food, taught us that God loves us more than birds and fields, in our best interests? If Jesus's purpose was to be a sacrifice for sin, why spend three years (or four depending on which gospel chronology you want to follow) teaching, healing, feeding, and setting people free from terrible things that afflicted them? Why not just do a few miracles to prove you are God, then announce you came to be a sacrifice for people's sin, and tell everyone to believe in you so that they can avoid eternal punishment by accepting your death in their place? The fact that Jesus never said anything of the sort is critical! If that was Jesus's mission, his purpose on earth, why not tell someone, anyone, especially his disciples?

Jesus's mission was to proclaim the kingdom of God was near, and he demonstrated and taught what that kingdom looked like: raising people from the dead (no death in God's kingdom), healing people (no sickness or disease in God's kingdom), feeding people (no scarcity in God's kingdom), eating with outcasts and those seen by polite society as "less than" (no social hierarchy in God's kingdom, everyone is welcome, is loved, and has a place). So what, then, is the gospel or good news of Jesus Christ?

I submit that Jesus came to remind us of what we had forgotten and missed in life, which is that we are all created in the image of love. This means we are to love God, others, and ourselves as God loves us. God is not a violent God of death, but of life. One of the early stories of both the Jewish and Christian faiths is that of Abraham and Isaac. God tells Abraham to sacrifice his only, beloved son, the son for whom he had waited twenty-five years. It seems odd to our modern ears, but child sacrifice would have been a common thing in Abraham's time. Abraham does as he is told and prepares to sacrifice Isaac, but as he raises the knife, an angel calls out to Abraham to stop! And a ram is provided for the sacrifice. The message of this story is that God is not a God of death and sacrifice. God is not like the other gods of the world. God is a God of life.

The lesson that Abraham took away from this heart-wrenching scenario was, "The Lord will provide" (Gen 22:14). God provides for life; God does not steal, kill, and destroy. God goes on to tell Abraham, "Because you have obeyed my voice, all the nations of the earth will be blessed" (Gen 22:18). This relationship between God and Abraham is special. In James 2:23, Abraham is characterized as "the friend of God." This deep and abiding relationship that Abraham and God had is the same relationship God desires with all humanity. And this friendship also illustrates something important about atonement.

One of the basic tenants of substitutionary atonement is that in order to be in relationship with God, one must accept Christ's sacrifice on their behalf. According to James 2:23, the only requirement to be a friend of God is to *believe* God. The Greek word used for "believe" in James 2:23 means "to put your trust in." In order to be in a deep and abiding relationship with God, one that allows God to consider you a friend, you must *trust* God. Even the apostle Paul twice references this idea of Abraham being credited with righteousness for trusting God, once in Romans 4:9 and again in Galatians 3:6. Both Paul and James are going back to Genesis 15:6 where God first promises to bless Abraham, the same blessing repeated after God provides the ram at the sacrifice of Isaac.

In Romans 4:9, Paul uses Abraham's trust in God as a way to show the Roman church that God intended to include the Gentiles in God's promise to Abraham through faith, by trusting in God. It is interesting that he adds at the end of Romans chapter 4 that we are to have the faith of Abraham, a faith that trusts in God *through the sacrifice of Jesus.* Paul is making a huge leap here and making faith in God all about trusting the sacrifice of Jesus to make us right before God. Paul is taking the Genesis scripture and making it say something it does not. Why does Paul do this?

We will discuss further in chapter 7, but in sum, Paul does this to show that the Gentiles, too, are to be included in the Abrahamic covenant. Just as Abraham trusted God, so too can the Gentiles through Christ. Abraham trusted God and this is what made him right before God. The message of Jesus all along was *trust God.* The message of James when he quotes the Genesis scripture is the same, be like Abraham and *trust God.* When Paul quotes the Genesis text again in Galatians, he is trying to convince the Galatian church not to listen to those he calls false apostles. The false apostles were Jewish Christians who were trying to convince the Gentiles in the Galatian church that they had to follow Jewish laws, like circumcision and dietary customs, in order to be considered true Christians. Paul says, "Not so!" It is by faith or trusting in God, like Abraham, that we are made right before God, not by trusting in the law. For Paul, the law which he had loved so dearly is now a curse and Jesus became a curse, so that the Gentiles might receive the blessing of Abraham and the Holy Spirit.

It seems as though Paul is confusing his own argument. Either it is by faith in God the Gentiles get included, or it is by the sacrifice of Christ. The reality is Paul is making an argument for inclusion and using the Jewish understanding of the Hebrew scriptures to prove his claim. Abraham is the father of the Jewish faith. Jesus is connected to Abraham by being the fulfillment of God's promise to Abraham. Therefore, one can achieve the trust in God Abraham had by having faith in Christ.

In Galatians 3:25–29, Paul says that by faith in Jesus we become children of God and by default also children of Abraham and heirs to God's promise to Abraham, the promise that we will possess the gate of our enemies and gain blessing for all the nations. The danger that has resulted in misunderstanding the claims of Paul, that access to God can be achieved through faith in Jesus alone, has led to the problem of supersessionism discussed earlier. Also called replacement theology, supersessionism has been the dominant view for much of church history. In 132 CE, Justin Martyr, an early church father, had a debate in Ephesus with a Jewish man named Trypho. In the debate, Justin proclaimed that the Old Covenant had passed away and that the Gentiles were the new Israel.[4] That was roughly only one hundred years after the resurrection of Jesus. That early in the Christian faith, leaders in the church were saying that Christians had replaced the Jewish people as God's own.

This is troubling because this view has led to the persecution of the Jewish people throughout history, including the Holocaust, where six million Jewish people were killed. I believe Paul would be horrified that his words were used to justify the killing of anyone, especially the Jewish people. Paul believed the mark of every true follower of Christ was love (I Cor 13 and Gal 5:22–23). In fact, Paul says in his letter to the Corinthian church that he is unfit to be called an apostle because he persecuted the church (I Cor 15:9). Why does Paul seem so angst-ridden and driven?

As we will discover later in chapter 5 on brain science, Paul's understanding of his faith in God in relation to the law was mapped to his brain so tightly that he had no identity outside of his work as a religious leader. In Philippians 3:4–6, Paul lists his accomplishments:

4. Martyr, "Dialogue with Trypho," chap. 11.

He was circumcised on the eighth day, a member of Israel, from the tribe of Benjamin, a Hebrew of Hebrews, a Pharisee of the law, zealous for what he believed, blameless when it came to following the Jewish law. This is how he saw himself, a very important man in the religious world of which he was a part. Then it all came crashing down. Imagine what it must have felt like to have Jesus appear to you on the road to Damascus. Suddenly everything you believed about yourself means nothing.

I think it was integral for Paul to reconcile what he believed all his life to this newfound faith in Jesus, including an understanding of Jesus as a substitutionary atonement. But just because Paul, and any other New Testament author, may have believed that Jesus was God's blood sacrifice (Romans 3:24–25), doesn't mean that is the way it is. There are many things in scripture that the majority of Christians do not believe. For instance, Numbers 5:11–31.

In Numbers, if a man becomes jealous of his wife, thinking that she has been unfaithful to him, he can take her before the priest with a grain offering. The priest will mess up the woman's hair, place the grain offering in her hands, then set her before the Lord. He will take holy water, mix it with dirt from the tabernacle floor and make her drink it. If she is innocent, nothing will happen to her. But if she has been unfaithful, the bitter water will cause her great pain and she will be unable to bear children. I have a friend who is a member of the very conservative African Methodist Church in Ghana and I asked him about this test for an unfaithful wife.

He and I had been in a spirited debate about the inclusion of LGBTQ persons in the church. He felt they should not be allowed in the church because he believed homosexuality was a sin against God. I did not believe this and supported full inclusion. His reason for excluding LGBTQ persons was because it was in the Bible. So I asked him about the bitter water test. First, he did not know this was in the Bible. Second, he said that if he suspected his wife of being unfaithful, he would not follow the Bible and make his wife drink dirty water. But, if someone chose to make their wife do this, they would not be going against God.

I include this story about my friend because it proves my point that we weight certain scriptures above others. To the question is substitutionary atonement necessary, my answer is no. There are many more scriptures we do not follow, such as those that say women should stay silent in church and ask their husbands later if they have questions about faith, or slaves should obey their masters as that is their duty in Christ. I believe the question can even be expanded to include all forms of atonement, to which my answer is again, no! Atonement is not necessary.

Atonement means to repay for wrongdoing. I hope I have laid out a reasonable argument that God does not require repayment for wrongdoing. God loves us and desires to be in relationship with us. Relationship, even if one-sided, does not require that the other party ask for forgiveness. It only requires that the offended party forgive. And God has done that. Over and over again in the Old Testament when the Hebrew people turned from God, God always provided a way back.

In the bizarre story of the prophet Hosea, God asks him to marry a prostitute named Gomer as a sign to the people that even though they are unfaithful, God will be faithful. Gomer continues to stray from Hosea as an adulteress and lover of other men (Hosea 3:1). Yet, Hosea continues to go after her and bring her back just as God remains faithful to bring the people back through steadfast love, mercy, and goodness (Hosea 2:19, 3:5). Jesus demonstrated this characteristic of God when he asked on the cross, "Father, forgive them for they know not what they do."

To the archaic definition of atonement, which means being at one or in harmony with one another, at-one-ment can be accomplished without death. In fact, I would argue you can't have harmony if death is required! Death ends any opportunity to make things right. You could argue death is the single biggest destroyer of human relationships. Even Jesus wept when he saw the heartbreak death caused to the ones he dearly loved (John 11:35).

If we go back to my premise that the gospel is "God loves us," then Jesus's mission becomes letting us know we are loved—not only loved as individuals, but brought into one big family of love. Jesus said his mother, brothers, and sisters were all those who do the will of God (Mark 3:35). If God is love and the fruit of God's Spirit or presence with us is love, joy, peace, patience, kindness, goodness, faithfulness, gentleness, and self-control (Gal 5:22–23), then the will of God is that we exhibit this same love and fruit in such a way that family is created.

In Acts 17:24–29, Paul proclaims God is the father of all humanity. We are all one big family with God as our Father. If this is the good news of Jesus, then the bad news, or sin, would be anything that attempts or fosters a separation of this kinship or a breaking of this family bond. Living without the fruit of the Spirit of love, joy, peace, kindness, goodness, faithfulness, gentleness, and self-control is a sure way to inflict harm and prevent family bonding.

The forgiveness of sin or justification before God would be our forgiveness for the harm we do to one another. Salvation then is the restoration of relationships with God and each other. Again, death is not required to bring about restored relationships. In fact, it is a contrite heart that is necessary for restoration to happen. In many churches on Ash Wednesday, when we remember our human frailty and that we will one day return to dust, Psalm 51 is read. Verse 17 says, "The sacrifice acceptable to God is a broken spirit; a broken and contrite heart, O God, you will not despise." The sacrifice acceptable to God is about a desire of the heart to be forgiven.

The idea that a death must take place to repay for wrongdoing is an eye for an eye type of justice. It is called the law of retaliation. Jesus said in Matthew 5:38–39, "You have heard that it was said, 'An eye for an eye and a tooth for a tooth.' But I say to you, Do not resist an evildoer. But if anyone strikes you on the right cheek, turn the other also." Jesus is reframing our need for retaliation and repayment. And Jesus himself did not use retaliation or violence in his life. Jesus resisted using violence to save himself. When Peter pulled out a sword and cut off the ear of the high priest's servant, Jesus said, "Put your sword back into its place; for all who take up the sword will perish by the sword. Do you think that I cannot appeal to my Father, and he will at once send me more than twelve legions of angels?" (Matt 26:52–53).

The human sin of wanting to use violence against each other puts us at odds with the God of love. Walter Wink, the theologian and biblical scholar mentioned earlier who was involved in the civil rights movement, believes God's redemption of humankind was necessary because humankind ultimately resents God and we use our free will to kill, leaving us unable to turn toward God.[5] He goes on to say, "God needs no reparation, but human beings must be extracted from their own prison if they are to be capable of accepting the pure gift of freely offered love. . . . It is not God who must be appeased, but humans who must be delivered from their hatred of God" and one another.[6]

Being delivered from hatred of God and others is embodied in Jesus's summation of the Law and Prophets as, "You shall love the Lord your God with all your heart, and with all your soul, and with all your mind. This is the greatest and first commandment. And a second is like it: You shall love your neighbor as yourself" (Matt 22:37–39). Atonement through sacrificial death is not necessary for us to love God, others, and ourselves. In fact, there is a certain level of self-hatred that must be present to believe that God cannot be in our presence or ours in God's because we are so sinful.

Lastly, I cannot talk about the gospel, sin, and salvation without addressing the wrath of God and the coming judgment by Jesus Christ. If there are parts of scripture we no longer follow like making wives drink dirty water out of fits of jealousy, do we conveniently neglect the parts of scripture that talk about wrath and judgment? Absolutely not! These things actually are pivotal to God's nature being one of love. Therefore, let us go into the next chapter: What about God's wrath and judgment?

---

5. Wink, *The Powers That Be*, 92.
6. Wink, *The Powers That Be*, 92.

Chapter 4
What about God's Wrath and Judgment?

Let no one deceive you with empty words, for because of these things
the wrath of God comes on those who are disobedient.
—Ephesians 5:6

The interesting thing in scripture about God's wrath and judgment is that it seems to be reserved for those who do not *live* rightly. Scripture never says it is reserved for those who do not *believe* rightly. Too often in Christianity, particularly with the theology of substitutionary atonement, we absolve ourselves of the commands to act justly, love mercy, and walk humbly with God because we believe Jesus died for our sins and has made us right with God. Jesus's death for sins becomes about a *transaction* between us and God instead of one that *transforms* us into people who act justly, love mercy, and walk humbly. So what are some of the things God's wrath is reserved for?

In Ephesians 5:6 and Colossians 3:6, God's wrath is coming on account of fornication, impurity, passion, evil desire, and greed, which is listed as idolatry. These are all about human behavior. Paul in his letter to the Roman church also communicates that the day of God's wrath will be to "repay according to each one's deeds" (Rom 2:6). No writer in the New Testament indicates—ever—that those who have accepted Jesus as their savior are exempt from judgment. Paul goes on to say, "There will be anguish and distress for everyone who does evil, the Jew first and also the Greek, but glory and honor and peace for everyone who does good. . . . For God shows no partiality" (Rom 2:9–11). God shows no partiality, even to those who claim to follow Christ.

In Matthew 25:31–46, Jesus is recorded as telling a parable about the nations of the world being judged as a shepherd separates sheep and goats. The basis on which this judgment comes is how the least are treated. Do you feed the hungry, give drink to the thirsty, clothe the naked, visit those in prison? Again, the judgment is about how one lives in relationship with others, not about right belief. In fact, Jesus says when these things are done, or not done, it is as unto him. Right belief in Jesus in this instance means believing he is in everyone you meet, especially those who need extra care.

Apparently, those who did not help the least also believed in Jesus, for they say, "Lord, when was it that we saw you hungry or thirsty or a stranger or naked or sick or in prison, and did not take care of you?" (Matt 25:44). They knew who Jesus was; otherwise, they would not have asked the question. According to this parable, God does not show partiality even to Christians. To be a Christian is to follow the example of Christ, who healed, set the oppressed free, welcomed the least, gave money to the poor, ate meals with anyone.

Then there is Luke's story of the faithful and unfaithful servant (Luke 12:41–48). A servant who is faithful is the one who does the work of his master. In this case, the faithful worker is the one who does the same things Jesus was doing. To this servant, it does not matter when his master returns, because he is busy doing what he has been asked to do. The unfaithful servant, on the other hand, beats the other servants and is only concerned with eating and getting drunk. Luke says the servant who knew what the master wanted, but didn't do it, will receive a severe beating. On the off chance there is a servant who was unclear about what the master wanted, so he didn't do what was expected, he will only receive a light beating.

It is obvious this is a story about being ready to face God. It is about punishment from God for our actions, knowing and unknowing. So it is easy to see how the penal substitutionary atonement theory came about in the sixteenth century. Scripture says God will punish. But what does severe beating versus light beating mean? And is it a one-time punishment, meaning the rest of eternity with God is one of peace and love with no more beatings required? I am not making light of these verses. I think these are legitimate questions, questions that a pastor once put into perspective for me.

I found myself going to a theologically conservative United Methodist Church when I was in my early thirties. The faith understanding of the church was very much one of Jesus being a substitute for our sins. And it also believed that homosexuality was wrong. I had wrestled with doubts about my salvation for years because I knew in my heart I was gay but could not admit it to myself out of fear. Once in college, when we were studying Revelation 20:11–15, which talks about the Book of Life being opened and those whose names were not found in it being thrown into the lake of fire, I immediately became concerned my name would not be in the book because I was gay! So I asked my Bible study leader if the verse was talking about losing your salvation. He answered, "The question isn't whether you can lose your salvation. It is why are you asking?"

The question felt like a trap. It was an extremely conservative college ministry and I felt that if I revealed to the group I was gay, I would have been told I needed to repent and not act on those feelings. Being plagued with doubt had not gone away in all the years since that college Bible study. Then while I was sitting in a church-wide Bible study at my conservative United Methodist Church, the pastor said, "God will definitely judge us, but you do not need to fear that judgment because God loves you." It was like a weight was lifted off of me. I suddenly no longer felt the nagging doubt and fear I carried for so long. First John 4:18, which says, "There is no fear in love, but perfect love casts out fear; for fear has to do with punishment . . .," suddenly took on new meaning for me. I no longer felt like I needed to worry about severe or light beatings. So if there is no fear in God's judgment, but God will judge us, what will that look like?

In the beginning of Revelation 21, the New Jerusalem descends from heaven and the announcement from the throne of God is that all pain and suffering have passed away, every tear is dried, and God will at last dwell with God's people. But then we have this: "Those who conquer will inherit these things, and I will be their God and they will be my children. But as for the cowardly, the faithless, the polluted, the murderers, the fornicators, the sorcerers, the idolaters, and all liars, their place will be in the lake that burns with fire and sulfur, which is the second death" (Rev 21:7–8). There are two questions I have from these verses.

The first is, who are the conquerors? The Greek word used here can be translated conquer, overcome, prevail, or get the victory. "Conquer" is a very militaristic word. But overcome, prevail, and get the victory imply that the conquerors are those who have endured the evils of the world and not lost their faith in God. This idea fits with the next verse, which says that the faithless or unbelieving will not inherit God's blessing of peaceful life together. So let's break down this list of who does not get to be called God's child or a conqueror. The words in parentheses are the different ways the original Greek can be translated.

In order to be God's child, one must avoid being:
- cowardly (fearful, faithless, timid),
- faithless (unbelieving, infidel, incredible thing, untrustworthy),
- polluted (abominable, abhorrent, disgusting, detestable),
- a murderer (always referring to a criminal and intentional homicide),
- a fornicator (whoremongers, libertines, a debauchee),
- a sorcerer (someone who gives spell-giving potions, a druggist, a pharmacist, a poisoner, a magician),
- an idolater (a servant or worshipper of an image),
- a liar (false).

There is nothing in the list that indicates a need to trust in the death of Jesus to pay for one's sins. You could say the "faithless" person is the one who doesn't believe Jesus died for his sins, but what if we were to use the word "infidel" instead of faithless? Does that change the meaning?

I have heard it argued that this list represents continual ways of being, not the occasional moment of unbelief, doubt, or lying, because we all have had moments of fear, doubt, and bending the truth. We most certainly have all visited a pharmacist! So what is the scripture really getting at? Should we shun murderers, cowards, and fornicators? What if we have been these, or still are? Are we excluded from God's kingdom? Is it a simple matter of believing Jesus is a substitute for the punishment I deserve for my actions? What if I am serving a life sentence for murder? Have I paid my debt to society, or must I also pay a debt to God?

I think it will be helpful to consider the verses right before the list of who isn't included. In these verses, the kingdom of God is described as having no more death, no more tears, no more pain. Murderers won't exist in the kingdom of God because there is no death. Liars won't exist in the kingdom because there is no more pain. Fornicators won't exist because there will be no sex in God's kingdom if we take Jesus at his word that we will be like the angels, neither marrying nor being given in marriage (Matt 22:30). We will all be brothers and sisters. The Greek word often translated as brothers and sisters in the New Testament means *siblings*. If we are all siblings in God's kingdom, we won't be having sex.[1]

The point is, all the things in the human heart that cause us to want to commit crimes, be cowardly, or be deceitful will be gone. The kingdom of God is the restoration of Eden, that place before the fall. Essentially, we are returned to the original state in which God intended for us to live. Every list of who will not inherit the kingdom of God in the New Testament is made up of those things that will no longer be present. The key is to separate actions from personhood. For instance, if you have a toddler who is enjoying finger painting and is getting totally covered in paint, you might say, "You are a mess!" Truthfully, that child is being messy, but they are not a mess in terms of their being. Ultimately, God does not define us by our actions. This is the good news! God loves us because we are God's children, not because of what we say or do.

You may recall at the beginning of the book, I shared that I started this journey of trying to understand atonement because of my own daughter. I love her with my whole being. If she were to commit murder (God forbid!), she would not cease to be my daughter, nor would I in any way stop loving her. If she went to prison, paid her debt to society, and was released, I would welcome her back into our home with open arms. This is the story of the prodigal son. No matter what we do with our lives, God is longingly looking for us, waiting for us to return. In order for the prodigal son to be welcomed back into his father's house, all he had to do was return. The beautiful thing about this story is that even before the son can get the words out to ask his father for forgiveness, the father runs out, throws his arms around his son, and begins kissing him.

---

1. For a deeper discussion about sexual ethics, I recommend listening to *The Liturgists Podcast: Ethics of F***ing (Parts 1 and 2)*, Season 4, Episodes 6 and 7 from April 5, 2018. Mike McHargue offers a framework of informed consent that goes beyond both people saying "yes." It is worth listening to.

Jesus didn't tell this parable only to leave out a crucial ending of the father requiring the son to offer a blood sacrifice in payment for his actions. The only sacrifice was the fatted calf for a celebratory meal, welcoming the son home again. Jesus left us another celebratory meal called communion. If you belong to a Christian community that partakes of the Lord's Supper, you have probably heard these words from I Corinthians 11:23–26:

> For I received from the Lord what I also handed on to you, that the Lord Jesus on the night when he was betrayed took a loaf of bread, and when he had given thanks, he broke it and said, "This is my body that is for you. Do this in remembrance of me." In the same way he took the cup also, after supper, saying, "This cup is the new covenant in my blood. Do this, as often as you drink it, in remembrance of me." For as often as you eat this bread and drink the cup, you proclaim the Lord's death until he comes.

The broken and bloodied body of Jesus that we are to remember in communion is not about punishment from God that Jesus endured in our place. His broken body and blood represent the fallen world in which we live where violence and death take place. These things are not part of God's kingdom. Look at the last verse above. We proclaim the Lord's death "until he comes" again. The Lord's death is not the end. Death does not have the final word. Life does. And we proclaim the end of death in communion, looking forward to Christ's return when God's kingdom of peace will be established.

So what about that lake that burns with fire and sulfur, which is the second death in Revelation 21:8? This brings me to my second question. If God will judge us for our actions, and those actions do not erase our being children of God, and we are not to fear God's judgment, what is the purpose of the lake of fire?

Sharon Baker, in her wonderful book *Razing Hell: Rethinking Everything You've Been Taught about God's Wrath and Judgment,* says that if God longs to be gracious and show compassion (Isaiah 30:18 is just one example among many others in scripture), then God's grace, love, and mercy also exist outside of temporal time.[2] In terms of judgment, in order for God to be consistent with God's character of graciousness and compassion, God's judgment must be for the purpose of reconciliation. In chapter 1, we defined reconciliation as restoring friendship or harmony between factions, or settling and resolving differences. If God's judgment is to restore friendship and harmony with us, to settle and resolve any differences we may have with God, then threatening to throw us into a lake of fire seems counter-productive.

Ultimately, if God is trying to help us see that the ways of violence, betrayal, lying, and fear that we have become so accustomed to in the world are not part of life in God's kingdom, then using violence would not prove God's point. The famous words of Rev. Martin Luther King Jr. prove this point well: "Darkness cannot drive out darkness; only light can do that. Hate cannot drive out hate; only love can do that."[3] Violence cannot drive out violence; only peace can do that. According to Baker, this means God's judgment is restorative.[4] There are two types of justice on which judgment can be based: restorative and retributive.

Restorative justice is just like it sounds. Its purpose is to restore the person and the relationships that have been damaged. Retributive justice is judgment for the purpose of retribution, or "an eye for an eye." It is punishment for wrongdoing. On the issue of an eye for an eye type of justice, Jesus said, "You have heard that it was said, 'Eye for eye, and tooth for tooth.' But I tell you, do not resist an evil person. If anyone slaps you on the right cheek, turn to them the other cheek also" (Matt 5:38–39). Jesus is taking the Old Testament law of retributive justice and saying, I give you a new command. Don't return violence for violence. Jesus is establishing God's restorative justice, a justice that offers peace, mercy, and compassion, not violence.

If God's desire is to end all evil, which includes violence, and all the things listed in scripture that will not be in the kingdom of God, then God will work to drive out those things through love. And what

2. Baker, *Razing Hell*, 146.
3. King, *Strength to Love*, 47.
4. Baker, *Razing Hell*, 18.

kind of love does God have? Deuteronomy 4:24 and Hebrews 12:29 both affirm that God is a consuming fire. Malachi 2:17—3:6 really brings this home:

> You have wearied the Lord with your words. Yet you say, "How have we wearied him?" By saying, "All who do evil are good in the sight of the Lord, and he delights in them." Or by asking, "Where is the God of justice?"
>
> See, I am sending my messenger to prepare the way before me, and the Lord whom you seek will suddenly come to his temple. The messenger of the covenant in whom you delight—indeed, he is coming, says the Lord of hosts. But who can endure the day of his coming, and who can stand when he appears?
>
> For he is like a refiner's fire and like fullers' soap; he will sit as a refiner and purifier of silver, and he will purify the descendants of Levi and refine them like gold and silver, until they present offerings to the Lord in righteousness. Then the offering of Judah and Jerusalem will be pleasing to the Lord as in the days of old and as in former years.
>
> Then I will draw near to you for judgment; I will be swift to bear witness against the sorcerers, against the adulterers, against those who swear falsely, against those who oppress the hired workers in their wages, the widow and the orphan, against those who thrust aside the alien, and do not fear me, says the Lord of hosts.
>
> For I the Lord do not change; therefore you, O children of Jacob, have not perished.

Malachi says the people have been asking, where is the justice of God? And the response is that a messenger is coming who will bring God's justice like a refiner's fire. Refining fire burns away impurities. Baker says that you can look at the lake of fire "as a lake of divine purification, a lake of cleansing so that the purified object (in our case, a person) can be dedicated and restored to God. . . . We can interpret the lake of fire as standing in the fiery presence of God," a fire that burns off all evil and sin, purifying us, destroying death within us, and restoring us to God.[5] This is the second death. Death to death.

Baker continues that once all the evil is destroyed, only the good image of God in which we were created will remain. And that goodness "would never reject God's offer of forgiveness and restoration."[6] I think it is important to point out the wording "God's offer." As an offer, we still get to choose whether or not we desire to be present in God's kingdom of peace and love. Just as God honors our right to choose evil or good, as in the example of Cain where God tells him to choose carefully because evil is lurking at his door, God maintains our freedom to choose in the end when we stand in judgment. But Baker contends, and I agree, that once we have been purified of all the evil and sin in our hearts, we will "naturally choose life with God. . . . 'He himself will be saved, yet so as through fire (I Cor 3:15).'"[7]

If we choose to view the lake of fire through this lens, we maintain that God is a God of love and justice, and one who respects human freedom. It also preserves the scriptures that point out all human beings will be judged for their behavior, regardless of belief. And lastly, if all humans will be judged and purified through God's all-consuming fire of love, then there is no need for substitutionary atonement. From this perspective, God accomplishes God's good and perfect will that none should perish (I Tim 2:4 and 2 Pet 3:9), and evil, sin, and death are destroyed once and for all, ushering in God's kingdom where there are no more tears and suffering. God's will prevails and every knee will bow and tongue confess that Jesus Christ is Lord (Rom 14:10–11, 2 Cor 5:10, and 1 Cor 3:13–15).[8] When we stand in the light of God's incomprehensible and extravagant love, God's judgment actually heals and provides forgiveness that was always there.

---

5. Baker, *Razing Hell*, 144.
6. Baker, *Razing Hell*, 144.
7. Baker, *Razing Hell*, 145.
8. Baker, *Razing Hell*, 165–66.

Chapter 5
Why Are We So Attached to Atonement?
(The Brain Chapter)

I praise you, for I am fearfully and wonderfully made.
Wonderful are your works; that I know very well.
—Psalm 139:14

In one of the churches where I served as youth minister, the youth group was charged with putting together a youth service for Sunday morning worship. The church was more traditional in its worship style with an organ, choir, and hymnals. But the youth decided they wanted a more contemporary style of worship with drums, guitars, etc., that reflected the type of music they enjoyed. They picked the story of David and Goliath, reading it as a metaphor for overcoming the giants in their lives. With this as the theme, we began to look for contemporary worship songs that would enhance it. One of the songs they picked had a lot of references to substitutionary atonement in it, things like "Jesus you took my place on the cross." So I changed the lyrics to not include a substitutionary reference.

Since we did not have a praise band in our church, I recruited a folk band that had performed at our church in the past. I emailed the music and lyrics to the band so they could practice and I made note of the lyrics that I had changed. A member of the band asked why the lyrics were changed. I explained that our church didn't believe in substitutionary atonement because it created a picture of God as a wrathful parent who is willing to allow their child to be killed for wrongdoing. For our congregation, God is a loving parent who forgives sin without needing punishment. We believed Jesus died because of sin, not for sin.

Another band member responded jokingly about using big seminary words like "substitutionary atonement." (All joking aside, he proves my point of why this book is necessary!) It is important to note here that pastors should explain why their congregations believe certain things and that other congregations do not hold similar views. It is okay for churches to believe differently. Discussing different theological views can actually strengthen people's faith if a culture and climate are created where it is healthy to discuss differing viewpoints. I did assume that the explanation email answered the question asked. But one should never assume when it comes to people's passionate views about belief. I was taught a valuable lesson about making assumptions.

The next morning I had three more emails from the band member that had been sent at 3:00 a.m. with long lists of scripture to prove to me that Jesus was the propitiation for our sins. In other words, Jesus's death satisfied and appeased God's wrath for sin. I gently replied to one email, not all three, that there are scriptures that indicate Jesus did die to appease God, but that is not a consistent view throughout all scripture. I encouraged him in his faith and let him know I was not trying to convince him of anything different from what he believed, only simply letting him know what our church believed. He did not send anymore emails, and he was wonderfully pleasant on the day of the youth worship service. But the incident did leave me wondering why people are so intent on their own way without any allowance that others might see things differently and still have a vibrant and life-giving faith in Jesus.

Not long after, I heard a podcast in which Sean Webb was being interviewed. He was talking about his book *Mind Hacking Happiness: The Quickest Way to Happiness and Controlling Your Mind.* After listening to him speak, I had to get his book. And sure enough, he answered my question of why people get so invested in only one way of looking at Jesus. He very entertainingly shares the medical and business research of various neuroscientists and university professors on how the brain works.

One study in particular was done by Dr. James Coan. In the study, Dr. Coan put participants in a functional magnetic resonance imaging (fMRI) machine that measures small changes in blood flow that occur with brain activity. This would allow them to read the subjects' brains in real time. The subjects were fitted with an ankle bracelet and a special pair of glasses that would flash a light. When the light flashed, they were told they would receive a small shock from the ankle bracelet. As suspected, the fear part of the brain lit up when the light flashed in anticipation of the shock.

In the second part of the experiment, another subject was brought in and placed in another fMRI machine next to the first person. The first subject was told that when the light flashed on their glasses, they would not receive a shock, but the other person would. Surprisingly, the fear part of the brain did not light up when the flash occurred because they knew they would not receive a shock. While this does raise some questions about human empathy and compassion for others, it confirms that, for the majority of people, we are for the most part concerned about ourselves. Now here is the interesting part of the final section of the experiment.

In the third part of the experiment, the first subject was told a loved one was brought in and placed in the fMRI machine next to them. This time when the light flashed, the fear part of the brain lit up even though they themselves were not going to receive a shock. What Dr. Coan concluded is that people whom we love become mapped to our brains. Essentially, our brains see them as extensions of ourselves.[1] Other researchers have followed up on Dr. Coan's work and determined that it is not only loved ones we see as extensions of ourselves, but things we love as well.

If you've ever wondered why sports fans will go out and break store windows and set cars on fire when their team loses, then here is your answer. Dr. Tiffany Barnett White at the University of Illinois researched people's reactions to different brands and determined that brand loyalty is actually the human brain extending its sense of self to that particular brand.[2] So if a brand fails or doesn't live up to its expectations, the brain sees that as a failure of self. This is the way the brain makes meaning out of the world. Our jobs, possessions, ancestry, national origin, and family can all become extensions of ourselves. It also is particularly true and powerful when it comes to things like sports,

---

1. Webb, *Mind Hacking Happiness,* 71–74.
2. Webb, *Mind Hacking Happiness,* 75.

politics, and religion.

Webb includes some findings from psychologists and neuroscientists that concluded "an attack on our strongly held beliefs is an attack on self . . . [including] our religious beliefs [which] also factor into our identities."[3] So if someone challenges a particularly long-held religious belief, like our particular view of atonement, we will see that as an attack on self. And the brain is designed to protect us. It is "your organ of survival."[4]

What this means is that, in the earliest days of human history, if a lion jumped out of the jungle and started heading toward you, your brain did not have time to think, "Oh, a lion is running toward me. What should I do? What are my best options to survive?" So the limbic system, or the primitive part of your brain, shut off the thinking part of your brain and took over, allowing you to run without thinking about it. This is your brain doing its job to protect you from a threat to self. But your limbic system does not distinguish between threats. It doesn't have time. So if someone challenges a deeply held belief, your limbic system sees that as a threat to self and will cause your body to react.

That reaction may be anger, which would have served you well in a violent culture where you might have to defend your life with a club or spear—or, in the world today, a gun. I think it is safe to say, we can do without these loaded kinds of defensive mechanisms in civil society. But our brains don't know that, no matter how smart we are. So why are we so attached to atonement? Because it has become mapped to our brains by going to church every Sunday as a child, or because it is what we were taught in Sunday school or by our parents or grandparents.

When I was in seminary, all first-year students were required to take a year-long class called *Spiritual Formation.* For the first semester, we had to write a weekly paper to explore where our concept of God had come from, what our experiences with God had been throughout our lives, and how seminary was affecting these concepts and experiences. Each week as I wrote, I began to realize that my concept of God had primarily come from the sermons that I had heard and secondarily from Christian authors whose books I had read. It was revelatory to discover

3. Webb, *Mind Hacking Happiness,* 77.
4. Webb, *Mind Hacking Happiness,* 69.

that there was no one way to see God. Even my reading of the Bible had been done through a particular way of seeing God that I had been taught.

This also is true of what we believe is the answer to the question, why did Jesus have to die? Here are some questions to help you think through where your concept of atonement came from: (1) What were you taught as a child about the death of Jesus? (2) Have you had that idea challenged by others or even yourself as you are thinking through your own faith? (3) Have you encountered different reasons for why Jesus died? If so, did any of those that were different from what you learned growing up resonate with you more? (4) What would you tell someone about Jesus who had never heard of him before?

These questions are a beginning point for thinking through why you believe what you do. And it matters. In Webb's book, he notes that anger and hate can become part of a person's identity.[5] When hate and anger get mapped to our brains as a way of making meaning out of the world, we stop striving for the common good and human welfare. The need for empathy and compassion also gets hijacked. Ultimately, when Jesus came to earth, this is what he was trying to teach us. Jesus summed up the law and the prophets with, "You shall love the Lord your God with all your heart, and with all your soul, and with all your mind. This is the greatest and first commandment. And a second is like it: You shall love your neighbor as yourself" (Matt 22:37–39). Without love, there can be no empathy and compassion.

Even Paul said everything hangs on love. In I Corinthians 13, the Love Chapter, Paul lists all the things that love is and is not. He concludes in verse 13, "And now faith, hope, and love abide, these three; and the greatest of these is love." James said loving your neighbor as yourself was "the royal law" (Jas 2:8). Taking what we've learned about the brain, you could easily define love as those we have mapped onto our brains and now see as an extension of ourselves. If we do this, then we would see all of humanity as an extension of ourselves. They truly would become our brothers and sisters, our family.

This is not new to Christianity. In Matthew 25:40, the gospel writer records Jesus as saying, "Truly, I tell you, just as you did it to

5. Webb, *Mind Hacking Happiness,* 149, 174.

one of the least of these *who are my family,* you did it to me" (*emphasis mine*). This scripture affirms all humanity is included in the family of God, with a special place for those who are excluded or considered the least. Human relationships are tied to relationship with God. What we do to one another we also do to God. Paul affirms this in his testimony of encountering Christ on the road to Damascus.

Acts 9:1–9 records Paul, while still known as Saul, approaching Damascus when light flashes all around him and he hears a voice say, "Saul, Saul, why do you persecute me?" Saul has no idea who is speaking and whom he is supposedly persecuting when he asks, "Who are you, Lord?" The reply is "Jesus." While Saul was persecuting those who followed the Way of Jesus, he would not have claimed to personally have been persecuting Jesus. To him, Jesus was a heretic who had stirred up a lot of trouble with Rome for the people of Israel. This interaction between the glorified Christ and Saul tells us that Jesus understood Saul's persecution of his followers to be direct persecution of himself. What was done unto the least was also done unto Jesus.

Not only does Jesus take the persecution of his followers personally, but he also indicates that he and his followers are one. This encounter was a powerful teacher for Saul who became Paul, not just because of the supernatural events surrounding it, or even the temporary blindness in which it resulted, but because it caused Paul to boldly state that there is no longer Jew or Greek, slave or free, male and female "for all of you are *one* in Christ" (Gal 3:28, *emphasis mine*). The oneness Paul preaches does not erase or eradicate the national origin, social class, or gender of humanity. It returns humanity to its original image of relationality, where we are all one family. Paul even rebukes Peter, the Rock, for his inability to recognize this family relationship of all humanity.

In Galatians 2:11–14, Paul tells of Peter, whom he calls Cephas, coming to Antioch where Paul confronts him for the apparent hypocrisy of openly treating the Gentiles as equals until some members of the Jerusalem Council come to Antioch and cast aspersions on him for eating with Gentiles. Paul feels compelled to confront Peter because he was not acting in consistency "with the truth of the gospel" (Gal

2:14). For Paul, the truth of the gospel was about the human family, the oneness of all humanity in Christ. For Peter, it reveals how his brain was doing what it was designed to do—protect him from being seen as outside his tribe. One of the ways our brain protects us is to keep us connected to those we have mapped to our brain as our tribe.

Tribal instincts are important for survival. The brain understands that we need to be connected to others to help us survive, from food sharing to protection from threats like animal and enemy attacks. It is what Shadyac discovered, mentioned in chapter 2. We need each other for survival. But this creates an "us"—those in our tribe—and a "them"—those outside our tribe. This separation between one another is what Jesus came to end, and God shows this to Peter in a very dramatic way.

In Acts 10, Peter has a vision of unclean animals being lowered three times before him with the Lord commanding him to kill and eat. Peter realizes God is telling him not to declare any human being unworthy of God's grace. Peter says, "I truly understand that God shows no partiality. . . . You know the message he sent to the people of Israel, preaching *peace* by Jesus Christ" (Acts 10:34–36, *emphasis mine*). Peace is to be the result of the ministry of Jesus. We cannot have peace until all people recognize we are all connected, we are all family. Unfortunately, the vision and understanding Peter received did not keep him from distancing himself from the Gentiles in Antioch. Peter's situation is not unique. We also continue to justify exclusion and separation due to ethnicity, cultural traditions, race, and gender.

Catherine Mowry LaCugna, a feminist theologian critical of the Catholic church for its continued insistence that women cannot serve as priests, says that together men and women represent the full image of God and it is the Christian hope initiated by Jesus that "in the reign of God, when all tears have been wiped away, women and men will no longer find themselves in the estrangement of 'otherness' but will be one in Jesus Christ, living together harmoniously. . . ."[6] The harmonious oneness between all of humanity, our oneness as family, is the hope Christians are to be demonstrating and offering to a world that continues to divide and separate. I believe those who have truly glimpsed this hope

---

6. LaCugna, *Freeing Theology,* 99.

become its greatest advocates. And this means consciously ending our brain's tribal hold on us!

Another aspect of our brain's design to keep us alive is its desire to conserve calories. As Mike McHargue says in *Finding God in the Waves,* our "brains are energy hogs."[7] Our brain uses an incredible amount of energy to keep us alive. So it is designed to conserve calories whenever possible just in case we go through a period when we won't have any calories to consume. It's programmed for survival. Donald Miller defines this survival mode as the "primitive desire we all have to be safe, healthy, happy, and strong. Survival simply means we have the economic and social resources to eat, drink, reproduce, and fend off foes."[8] This means our brains don't like to spend a lot of time figuring things out. They want to keep it simple.

Atonement theories help keep it simple. I was invited to teach a Sunday school class at a local church on the different theories of atonement. Many of the class members had come from evangelical non-denominational backgrounds, had deconstructed their faith, and were in the process of reconstructing their faith. When I mentioned that penal substitutionary atonement was the dominant view in the United States, many nodded their heads and affirmed that this is the view they were taught. But then one person cautiously raised her hand and asked, "Why is it the dominant view?"

This is where brain science is particularly helpful. If you were raised in a conservative Christian church, you are probably familiar with the bridge illustration. I was taught it as part of the Navigators Christian Fellowship group in college. As part of our commitment to this campus fellowship group, we went door to door in dorms sharing the gospel with people. (I confess, this was an awful experience and I only did it once.) And the gospel was presented through the bridge illustration. It goes like this:

Humanity sinned against a holy God. This sin separated us from God, creating a vast canyon between us and God. We cannot cross over to God on our own merit. We will die in our sins and go to hell for eternity unless we accept by faith that Jesus died for our sins. The cross

7. McHargue, *Finding God in the Waves,* 64.
8. Miller, *Building a Story Brand,* 51.

on which Jesus died creates a bridge for us to cross over to God where we can enjoy eternity with God.

This is a very simple illustration and I believe the answer to why penal substitutionary atonement is so popular. It is easy to understand and very succinctly solves the problem of sin and answers the question of why Jesus died. The brain likes simplicity. We have a problem (sin); God provided a solution (Jesus's death on the cross); we accept God's answer to our problem (forgiveness); and everything is fine between us and God. No worries. In actuality, though, sin is much more complicated than our individual issues. It can create wars and genocide. We can't forget that it was those who proclaimed to be Christians who started the Crusades that lasted from 1095 to 1492, killing thousands in the name of Jesus. It was Christians who killed the native Americans and took their land. It was Christians who justified slavery with scripture and entered into the buying and selling of human beings.

While the brain may seek out simplicity in the beginning, I do not believe it can stay there. Because our brains are designed to change with new experiences, the more we encounter and spend time with those we see as being in another tribe, the more we will begin to truly live out the gospel, which is to connect to each other as family. A gospel that allows us to check off boxes to satisfy our brains does not honor the life, death, and resurrection of Jesus. It was a lot of hard work that Jesus put into teaching and healing people. He wore himself out, so much so, he fell asleep in a boat and even a mighty storm didn't wake him (Matt 8:23–27, Mark 4:35–41, Luke 8:22–25). That's some serious exhaustion! The gospel cannot be narrowed down to just be about sin and Jesus's death on the cross. It is much bigger than that. It encompasses the whole of creation. In Romans 8:19–23, Paul said even creation is groaning for release from decay and awaits the glorious freedom God provides. So let's help our brains create new neural pathways that encompass all of humanity as our brothers and sisters.

Chapter 6
What About Atonement in the Old Testament?

He shall do with the bull just as is done with the
bull of sin offering; he shall do the same with this.
The priest shall make atonement for them; and they shall be forgiven.
—*Numbers 4:20*

In this chapter, we will consider the Old Testament ritual of temple sacrifice in Israel's history and how this directly affects the views of the atoning work of Jesus. If blood sacrifice was indeed how God primarily atoned for sin in the Old Testament, then Jesus as the necessary blood sacrifice for the sin of all humanity falls in line with the dominant Western view of substitutionary atonement. But was animal sacrifice the primary way in which God forgave the Hebrew people of their sins? We have already looked at how God turned away from destruction when reminded of God's friendship to Abraham. So why did animal sacrifice to God begin?

You could say God was the first to institute animal sacrifice as a result of sin in Genesis 3:21. The scripture says that God made garments of skin for the man and his wife. The Hebrew word for "skin" in this text means animal hide or leather. When the earth creature, the meaning of "Adam" in Hebrew, disobeyed God and ate of the tree of death, God removed Adam and Eve from the garden of God so that they would not eat of the tree of life. So God covered their nakedness with animal hides of leather. Certainly God could create animal skins out of nothing, but seeing as death has entered into existence, it would seem appropriate that it is through the death of an animal the people are clothed.

Immediately following the expulsion from the garden, Cain and Abel are born in Genesis 4:1–2. Cain is said to till the land and Abel raises sheep. In verse 4, Abel brings an offering to God of animal fat, which pleases God. There is no official command recorded that an offering be made to God in any form, but Abel's offering of animal fat from the first of his flock pleases God. Some scholars believe that Abel's offering was not a result of him killing the animal, but that the animal fat is milk. If this is the case, then it would not be until after the flood that an animal sacrifice with blood is offered, in Genesis 8:20. After Noah, his family, and all the animals exit the ark, Noah builds an altar and sacrifices animals and birds, pleasing God, causing God to say in God's heart that never again will humankind be destroyed by God. In Genesis 8:21, just before the vow not to destroy humanity again, God acknowledges the evil in human hearts. This is an important recognition and pronouncement.

If we return to chapter 4 and the lake of fire being God's purifying love, which purifies humanity of the evil in the human heart and ultimately destroys death once and for all, then God remains faithful to the promise following Noah's sacrifice. There is a precedent set here by Noah that blood sacrifice does change God's heart regarding human evil. But according to God's decision, the destruction of humanity because of human evil will not take place again. This means Jesus's sacrifice as an atonement for human sin would be unnecessary by God's own word.

The next significant sacrifice in Genesis is the offering of Isaac. We discussed this in a previous chapter, but it is worth noting again that both human and animal sacrifice was a common practice in the ancient world. So it is not a surprise that blood sacrifice is part of the Old Testament narrative without explanation. In Exodus, instructions for burnt offerings and the building of the altar to perform such sacrifices are given. In terms of atonement, the most notable scripture is Exodus 25:27, in which God tells Moses that it is above the mercy seat (in chapter 7, the mercy seat will be discussed further) that God will meet with the priest. It is when we get to Leviticus that we have specific instructions that animal blood sacrifice will serve as an atonement for the sins of the people.

In the first four chapters of Leviticus, we have instructions for burnt offerings, grain offerings, well-being offerings, and sin offerings. As those most related to our discussion of substitutionary atonement, let's look at the sin offering instructions in Leviticus 4. For sins committed by the people, both knowingly and unknowingly, the elders of the congregation are to lay their hands on the head of a bull, then slaughter it in the presence of the Lord. The priest then makes the atonement for the people. There are several points to consider in terms of Christian substitutionary atonement.

First, Jesus is referred to as the "Lamb of God" in the New Testament twenty-nine times, most notably by John the Baptist when he says, "Here is the Lamb of God who takes away the sin of the world!" (John 1:29). The animal used as a sin offering in the Levitical law is a bull, not a lamb. In Leviticus 4:32, if a lamb is brought as a sin offering, it is to be a female. Jesus was male. This may seem like I am splitting hairs. What I hope we realize is that justifying Jesus as a substitute sacrifice to God for human sin is not a one-to-one wash with Old Testament law.

Jesus's identification as a lamb is more closely related to the Passover lamb. The Passover lamb was to be without blemish and slaughtered so that its blood could mark the doorposts of the Israelites. The mark was an indication that the spirit of death should pass by those living there. There was no transfer of guilt and sin to the lamb. It was purely about death passing over the Israelites. This follows our discussion in earlier chapters that God is a God of life, not death. God's desire is to preserve and save life.

Second, Jesus is identified as our high priest (Heb 2:17; 4:14). His role is one of offering the atonement, not being the sacrifice. The Hebrew word for "atonement" used in Leviticus means to appease, cleanse, forgive, be merciful, pacify, pardon, and make reconciliation. Certainly, the people of Israel understood God to have forgiven them when they completed the required ritual. The ritual itself was just that, a symbolic act recognizing that individually and corporately the people had sinned, so that they would understand God had forgiven them. The purpose was not that their actual sin was transferred to the animal so that they may be forgiven. To make sure I was on the right track in thinking this, I met with Anjelica Ruiz, Director of Libraries and Archives at Temple Emanu-El in Dallas, Texas, the largest synagogue in the Southern United States.

Ruiz holds multiple degrees, is a member of the Anti-Defamation League's Glass Leadership Institute and sits on their regional Texoma board. She is also a member of the JewV'Nation Fellowship Jews of Color cohort as well as a teacher of Judaica, things pertaining to Jewish life and customs, especially when of a historical, literary, or artistic nature, as books or ritual objects. She is well accredited to answer questions pertaining to Jewish life surrounding atonement.

Ruiz explained that atonement in the Jewish tradition is all year round and the purpose is seeking forgiveness. Individuals who have sinned against another must go to the person they have wronged and ask for forgiveness. The person who has been wronged is not required to forgive. Sins against God are confessed together as a community with the belief that the people are not alone in their sin. Everyone is in it together. In terms of ancient Judaism and the ritual of animal sacrifice, Ruiz offered it has never been part of their tradition to believe the sins of the people were physically transferred to the animal, the reason being that the purpose of asking for forgiveness of God or another person is to take responsibility for your actions. You cannot transfer your responsibility.

This directly relates to substitutionary atonement, which is transferring one's responsibility to Jesus instead of taking ownership for one's actions. If one subscribes to the Western view that sin is genetic, then one cannot take responsibility for a genetic condition. It would be something they would have no control over. But the Judaic view, as presented by Ruiz, is that sin is not genetic. It is a result of human free will. When a person chooses evil, they are to ask for forgiveness from the person or persons they have wronged. This is seen as repairing the world and this work is the responsibility of every person. Ruiz shared this quote from the *Pirkei Avot*, which means "Sayings of the Fathers" or "Ethics of the Fathers" and is from the Mishnah, an early collection of oral sayings that has been passed down through generations: "You are not responsible to finish the work of repairing the world, but you cannot turn away from it."

The idea of atonement in the Jewish tradition is about restoration of relationships between individuals and together with God. It is a continual work from which one cannot shirk their responsibility. Really, God is not after sacrifices and burnt offerings, but relationship. Consider these Old Testament verses:

> **Psalm 40:6–8** "Sacrifice and offering you do not desire, but you have given me an open ear. Burnt offering and sin offering you have not required. Then I said, 'Here I am; in the scroll of the book it is written of me. I delight to do your will, O my God; your law is within my heart.'"

> **Isaiah 1:11** "What to me is the multitude of your sacrifices? says the Lord; I have had enough of burnt offerings of rams and the fat of fed beasts; I do not delight in the blood of bulls, or of lambs, or of goats."

> **Jeremiah 7:21–22** "Thus says the Lord of hosts, the God of Israel: Add your burnt offerings to your sacrifices, and eat the flesh. For in the day that I brought your ancestors out of the land of Egypt, I did not speak to them or command them concerning burnt offerings and sacrifices."

> **Hosea 6:6** "For I desire steadfast love and not sacrifice, the knowledge of God rather than burnt offerings."

These verses indicate that animal sacrifice was never God's full intent. It was in some ways akin to what Paul said about the law. It was something that served a purpose but, once fulfilled, pointed us to greater reality—in this case, relationship with God.

The beginning of the Jewish New Year is Rosh Hashana and is ten days before Yom Kippur, which is the Day of Atonement on the Jewish calendar. These are high holy days for the Jewish people, called the Ten Days of Awe. During these days leading up to the Day of Atonement, the people are expected to be searching their hearts for where they have wronged others and begin seeking forgiveness from those individuals. On Yom Kippur, the people gather as one to confess their sin and ask for forgiveness from God, and the rabbi pronounces them clean. It also is on this day that the Book of Life is opened at the beginning of Yom Kippur and closed at the end. There is no literal adding or erasing of names. According to Ruiz, it symbolizes the act of seeking reconciliation, which is what the Ten Days of Awe and Yom Kippur are all about.

Once the people are proclaimed purified by the rabbi, it is seen as an opportunity to start over, to start fresh, to make things new. For Jesus to be the atoning sacrifice of all people, he is providing for us the opportunity to start fresh again and again in the work of forgiveness and choosing good. It was never about a single pronouncement that you are forgiven so that you can now go to heaven and nothing more is ever required. Jesus as high priest tears the separating curtain between humanity and God, forgiving us of our sin so that we engage in the work of repairing the world with God. I like to look at it this way: Jesus came to show us what God's kingdom looks like, a place where people are forgiven, healed, and free. And that forgiveness, healing, and freedom is *continual.* It was not a one-time thing accomplished on the cross.

In summary, the Day of Atonement in the Old Testament was the holiest of days when the temple priest made animal sacrifice for the sins of the people for the entire year. But the purpose of the Day of Atonement was not for the people to have their sin wiped away in order for them to continue living as they had before. The Day was marked by significant prayer, fasting, and rest. It was a time of self-reflection in order that personal change might take place, that the sin lurking at the door might be mastered. As said in Hosea 6:6, God desires mercy, not sacrifice. It is a change of heart desired by God, not the blood sacrifice. The blood was symbolic of a transformed heart and life that repairs the world.

Chapter 7
How Is Atonement Addressed in the New Testament?

They are now justified by his grace as a gift,
through the redemption that is in Christ Jesus,
whom God put forward as a sacrifice of atonement by his blood,
effective through faith.
—Romans 3:24–25

There are three ways in which I want to look at atonement in the New Testament. First, we will look at what the four gospels say about atonement. Second, we will address Paul's writing. Third, we will consider a few other books of the New Testament. Before we dive in, I feel like we need to watch a safety video like the ones they make you watch before your child can jump at a trampoline park. Only, our safety video needs to be about allowing ourselves grace as we wrestle with the scriptures. It also needs to explain that the New Testament writers, including Paul, were not systematic theologians. If you recall from the first chapter, a systematic theology is when you believe one thing, say for instance about sin, then logically what you believe about salvation must remedy what you view sin to be.

The reality is that most of us are not systematic theologians either. We don't read the Bible thinking, "Oh, I believe sin is breaking the ten commandments. So when I did not honor my mother and father by taking the trash out when they asked, I know that I am forgiven because Jesus died for my sin." When we read scripture, we tend to read it pastorally, meaning Jesus is like my pastor. Jesus is the one I look to for guidance about how the Bible applies to my life. Or we read it incarnationally, meaning that just as Jesus was the incarnation, or image of God on the earth (Heb 1:3), we read it to be *transformed* by God. This means the Bible must be read in concert with the Holy Spirit, so that the

Spirit of God can open our eyes. The incarnation also reveals, and the Spirit confirms, the importance of the human experience and the value God places on human lives.

This is an important part of our safety video. Scripture is not about bringing our human experience and trying to figure out how it fits into first-century Christianity. Reading scripture is an experience with God's Spirit, revealing how our lives can better reflect God's image in the world we live in today. This might sound like the same thing, but it isn't. The Bible isn't a rule book to tell us what to do in every situation. It is, as Peter Enns says in *How the Bible Actually Works*, a book of contradictions that invites us into wisdom, to think through how God is working in the world and how we can be a part of it.[1]

And that makes more sense. We encounter things every day, like cell phones, that we have to make decisions about. Do I spend too much time on my phone? Do I override the time limit I set on Facebook? Do I let my fifth-grader have a phone because all of his friends do? First-century Christians never had to think about these questions, but the Holy Spirit can lead us to a scripture like Ephesians 5:15–16, "Be careful then how you live, not as unwise people but as wise, making the most of the time, because the days are evil." After reading this, you may decide that 30 minutes a day is plenty of time on Facebook, especially if certain posts make you grumpy and angry.

The fruit of the Spirit—love, joy, peace, patience, kindness, goodness, faithfulness, gentleness, self-control—is the opposite of grumpy and angry. Both the fruit of the Spirit and being grumpy and angry can be transformational, but one is positive and one is more negative. In terms of how our lives can better reflect God's image in the world, which is a better reflection—the fruit of the Spirit or being grumpy? Now, which of these images is more reflective of the fruit of the Spirit—a God who demands a payment for sin or a God who freely gives simply because we are God's children? I wager it is God's abundant grace freely given that reveals a gospel of love. I believe this is what the gospel writers were trying to communicate about the death of Jesus. Let's look now at the gospels.

---

1. Enns, *How the Bible Actually Works*, 31–34.

MATTHEW

In Matthew 1, an angel appears to Joseph and tells him in a dream not to be afraid to take Mary as his wife, for the child she is carrying "will save his people from their sins" (Matt 1:21). The Greek word used for "save" in this verse also is used seven more times in Matthew (8:25, 14:30, 16:25, 18:11, 27:40, 42 and 49). It means the same thing in all seven references—to deliver, protect, heal, preserve, do well, make whole. The angel didn't say to Joseph that Jesus would die for his people's sins. He said Jesus would protect the people from their sins, give them wholeness for their sins. No death is implied or needed for Jesus to make this happen. Instead, the word used in verse 21 implies God's shalom, God's peace that surpasses all understanding.

To be clear about what Matthew means, we can look at Jesus's words in Matthew 11:28, "Come to me, all who are weary and heavy-laden, and I will give you rest." The Greek word for "rest" means refresh. Jesus came to refresh people, to lift their burden caused by sin. He never said, "I have come to remove people's sins by dying for them." Jesus is not recorded as saying he came to remove people's sin. Instead, he repeatedly assures people he came to restore, renew, give life to them because life was hard enough, especially under Roman rule. Jesus also was concerned with the burdens the religious leaders of his day were placing on the people (Matt 23:4).

I don't know about you, but to me that is good news for today—to know that when we struggle to pay bills or be good parents, good employees, good followers of Jesus Christ, or when religious leaders do harm instead of good, Jesus comes to refresh, to lighten burdens. He does not come to proclaim us estranged from God because of sin, or even more stressful, because we need someone to pay a debt of blood in our place. This type of understanding of God does not bring me peace. I believe Matthew is communicating to us that Jesus came to give us God's peace, not to pay a debt. Then you may be thinking, "Why then did Matthew say in 20:28 'the Son of Man did not come to be served, but to serve, and to give his life a ransom for many'?"

Ransom sounds a lot like a payment. And that is exactly what the Greek word there means: a redemption price, an atonement, something with which to set free. I am sure this is where the idea for the Ransom Theory came about—Jesus came to give his life as a redemption price for many. But we have to look at the verse in terms of what Jesus is telling the disciples. In Matthew 20:24–27, he tells them that they are not to rule over others or be tyrants, but are to be servants of all. Jesus says he himself did not come to lord his position over people. He came to serve. Here is where it is important to look at a very famous hymn that was most likely very familiar to Matthew's community of Christians.

In Philippians 2:1–11, Paul quotes a hymn about Jesus. It is called the *Philippian Hymn* or *Christological Hymn,* and it was probably sung in the majority of the early Christian churches. Paul used it because it would have been familiar to the church in Philippi. The hymn says that Jesus found himself in the form of a slave. The Greek word used here for "slave" is the lowest possible form of a slave, someone who was sold into slavery because they could not pay a debt or were a slave due to being a prisoner of war. These individuals typically lived very hard lives and were an essential part of the Roman economy, even though they had no rights of their own.

Matthew is reminding his community of faith through the words of Jesus that he came to be like them, perhaps even lower, a slave with no rights. When Jesus says in Matthew 20:28 that he gives his life a ransom, he is saying, "I give my life as a slave, the lowest form of a slave, with no rights, to serve many." He is not saying his life is a payment for wrongdoing. He is saying his life is that of a servant. He is the servant God who has come to set people free from the weariness and heaviness of life, to bring them joy and peace in the midst of harsh realities. Matthew most likely lifted this scripture word for word from Mark 10:45.

Mark is the earliest of the gospels, written somewhere around 60–75 CE. Matthew was written about twenty years later in 80–90 CE. The majority of modern Bible scholars agree that Matthew relied heavily on Mark as he was writing his gospel, using about 80 percent of Mark. I point this out because it is unlikely that Matthew intended his use of the word "ransom" to mean anything different from Mark. They both understood Jesus to mean his life was given in service to many as a slave.

MARK

The gospel of Mark uses the word "saved" five times in reference to what God is doing. In Mark 10:26, the disciples ask, "Who then can be saved?" when Jesus says it is difficult for the rich to enter the kingdom of God. The Greek word for "saved" is the same as used in Matthew. It is *sozo* and means deliver, protect, heal, preserve, make whole. For our discussion, the question could be phrased, "Who then can receive atonement?" If making payment for a wrong is what salvation means, then the disciples hit the nail on the proverbial head! Surely the rich can make payment for their wrongdoing. I am sure they can. But Jesus simply looked at them and said, "For mortals it is impossible, but not for God; for God all things are possible."

Jesus did not say that atonement would be made by him. He is reassuring the disciples that being forgiven by God and being part of God's kingdom is not about how much money someone has. God will forgive them. This is possible for God! And not only forgive them, but make them whole, give them God's peace that surpasses all understanding. It is no surprise that the disciples had difficulty comprehending this. We have difficulty comprehending it today, too. The fact that God willingly forgives us and does so without any hesitation seems fantastical. But Jesus came to assure us it is not.

Before we leave the gospel of Mark, I wish to look at Mark 14:24, in which Jesus is sharing Passover with the disciples before his impending arrest, trial, and death. He says, "This is my blood of the covenant, which is poured out for many." Again, this is not about blood sacrifice for sins. Jesus is instituting the kingdom of God, a new way of living. A covenant is not like a contract. Contracts are legal transactions that are binding on all parties involved, and everyone involved must fulfill their obligations in the contract. A covenant, on the other hand, is based on relationship. It is a vow between parties made in good faith. Jesus's reference to this new covenant being made in blood is probably in reference to the Abrahamic covenant of old, made between God and Abraham, a covenant vow that was sealed by cutting a heifer, goat, and ram in two pieces and a flaming torch and smoking firepot passing between the pieces (Gen 15).

Passing between the bloody animal pieces signified the covenant. Jesus knew he was going to die. His blood would not be shed in vain. Let his blood be a sign of a new covenant with God, one based on the kingdom of God, where people serve one another. Jesus's foreknowledge of his death is not an endorsement of his needing to die. The shedding of his blood was not necessary to enforce the covenant. The covenant, like the one with Abraham, is about abiding relationship. God does not need sacrifice, let alone human sacrifice, to do God's will. As we discussed in the story of Abraham and Isaac, God is not like the other gods that need human sacrifice.

It is no wonder that we have made Jesus's death all about blood and sacrifice for sin instead of a sign for us to give up violence and serve one another in love as the lowest of the low. It is our inclination toward sin that keeps us from wanting to truly serve and see others better than ourselves. It is with this in mind that we now turn our attention to the gospel of Luke. He had an interesting understanding about the death of Jesus.

LUKE/ACTS[2]

The story of Zacchaeus can sum up the whole of how Luke viewed salvation and the death of Jesus. In Luke 19:1–10, Jesus invites himself to stay at the home of Zacchaeus, a "sinner" as he was called by all who saw Jesus go with him. During Jesus's stay, Zacchaeus has a transformation of heart and offers to give half his possessions to the poor and repay with interest any money he has gotten through fraud. Jesus says, "Today salvation has come to this house, because he too is a son of Abraham. For the Son of Man came to seek and save the lost."

The Greek word used for "salvation" in this passage means to deliver, rescue, bring safety and health. It is God's abundant life. Jesus follows up this statement by restating his mission: to seek and save the lost. The Greek word for "save" is again *sozo*, to preserve and make whole. According to Luke, God's salvation is all about a change of heart that causes one to live in a manner worthy of the kingdom, by caring for the poor and living as a servant to others. Salvation is not Jesus dying for sins.

---

2. I am including the book of Acts in the discussion of the gospel of Luke since they were written by the same person.

Greg Carey, professor of New Testament at Lancaster Theological Seminary, says, "For Luke, Jesus' death carries no saving power on its own. It provides no atonement for sins. . . . Instead, Jesus dies as a consequence of his commitment to bless all people, especially the poor and sinners."[3] According to Carey, Luke provides a distinctive understanding of Jesus's death: "Jesus dies just as he lived, seeking the blessing of others, especially sinners and the disadvantaged."[4] And in both Luke and Acts, "whenever Jesus' disciples preach the good news, they discuss Jesus' execution as a horrible crime—and then they announce the good news of Jesus' resurrection."[5]

It's true. In Acts 2:23, when Peter is preaching to the people after Pentecost, he refers to "this man . . . you crucified and killed." Jesus's death is always presented as a crime and a terrible loss. When the people hear Peter's preaching, they are cut to the heart and ask what they must do (Acts 2:37). Peter responds, "Repent, be baptized every one of you in the name of Jesus Christ so that your sins may be forgiven. . . ." (Acts 2:38). Repentance, or asking for forgiveness, is the key to having your sins forgiven. Luke does not say, "Accept the death of Jesus on your behalf." Following the mass baptism where 3,000 people believed after Peter's sermon, the people devoted themselves to learning, being in community with one another, eating together, and praying. It is a picture of the kingdom of God, a picture similar to the one John paints for us in his gospel.

JOHN

John is not like the other three gospels. The gospels of Matthew, Mark, and Luke are called synoptic gospels because they give a general summary or *synopsis* of the life, death, and resurrection of Jesus. John is more like poetry, opening with the famous words, "In the beginning was the Word, and the Word was with God, and the Word was God" (John 1:1). John does not give us a summary of Jesus's life, death, and resurrection. He grounds Jesus as co-eternal with God and active with God in the creation of the world as well as all life residing in Jesus. I

---

3. Carey, "Luke's Interpretation of Jesus' Death," para. 3.
4. Carey, "Luke's Interpretation of Jesus' Death," para. 7.
5. Carey, "Luke's Interpretation of Jesus' Death," para. 8.

think it is safe to say that John views God's abundant life as the kind of life demonstrated by Jesus. Just as we looked at the story of Zacchaeus for the key understanding of Luke's assessment of salvation, John provides a key passage to sum up his assessment of the death of Jesus.

In John 3:14–15, Jesus tells Nicodemus that "just as Moses lifted up the serpent in the wilderness, so must the Son of Man be lifted up, that whoever believes in him may have eternal life." Jesus is referring to Numbers 21:4–9, where the people have been complaining against God and Moses. As a result, serpents begin to come out of the woodwork and bite people, causing them to die from poisonous bites. They repent of their speaking against God and Moses and ask for help. Moses is instructed by God to place a bronze serpent statue on a pole and lift it up high in the camp so when someone is bitten by a snake, they can look up at the bronze snake sculpture and be saved from the bite.

It's a strange story. It seems that over time, people began to worship this snake statue. In 2 Kings 18:4, it says that King Hezekiah had to tear down and break into pieces this serpent that Moses had made because the people named it Nehushtan and were worshipping it. Why did Jesus reference this story in relation to himself? The prevailing wisdom of the Christian church is that it represents Jesus being lifted up on the cross. Looking at Jesus on the cross would bring belief in Jesus, resulting in eternal life. This sounds a lot like Jesus's death having saving power. Is this why Jesus used this bizarre story?

First, we have to consider John's style in writing. In this chapter, John continually uses symbolism—Nicodemus comes to Jesus in darkness (3:2) while Jesus is the light of the world (3:19); people must be born of water and Spirit (natural birth and spiritual birth) (3:5–6); the wind blows but you cannot see it like those born of the Spirit (the Greek words for "wind" and "spirit" are the same) (3:8); Nicodemus also represents a particular Jewish way of understanding God. John is presenting Jesus as the way to understand God. The serpent story functions like this also. In the Old Testament, the serpent statue led to idolatry and had to be destroyed. Jesus references the serpent story because he is presenting a way of understanding God, one that does not lead to idolatry, but the life that God intends for all people. The

Reverend Alexis Chase, the vicar from Holy Comforter Episcopal Church in Atlanta, Georgia, has an additional understanding of this text that is helpful.

Chase believes what is interesting about John's inclusion of the serpent story "is that the Israelites, in order to be saved from death, they had to look upon the symbol of their sickness—they had to look at what was causing their own death."[6] This goes well with John's testimony that the people loved the darkness more than the light (3:19). It is the darkness of their evil deeds that causes the death of Jesus. The people seeing Jesus hanging on the cross must be faced with their own darkness, the very thing that caused Jesus to be crucified in the first place. It is similar to the Scapegoat Theory of atonement, in which Girard says in the death of Jesus we see our own tendency toward violence. John uses the serpent story to point out that, in Jesus, God must be understood as one that does not endorse the evil deeds of darkness.

Salvation or eternal life is not about Jesus dying for sins so people can go to heaven. For John, it is about seeing Jesus and seeing God at the same time: "Whoever has seen me has seen the Father" (John 14:9). This way of seeing God leads us to eternal life, which is to live out the new commandment to love one another as Jesus has loved us (John 15:12). John uses a play on words again to illustrate this in John 15:2–3.

These verses tell us that God is the vinegrower who prunes the branch so it bears more fruit. The Greek root word for "pruning" is the same as "cleansing." Jesus says that the word has cleansed them, the word being the *logos* mentioned in John chapter 1. *Logos* in Greek means not just the spoken word itself, but the intent behind the word, the reason it is spoken. Jesus as the *logos* is the expression of God, the intent of God. That intent or reason for Jesus's coming was not to be a sacrifice for sin, but that we be born anew of God's Spirit as children of God who love like Jesus.

John also holds claim to the most famous verse in the Bible, John 3:16. In John 3:16, John says God loved the world so much that God sent Jesus. It is verse 17 that gives us context for verse 16: "For God did not send the Son into the world to condemn the world, but in order that

---

6. Chase, "3/15/15 — 4th Sunday in Lent," para. 6.

the world might be saved through him."[7] John makes clear that Jesus came to save the world. The word for "saved" in 3:17 is *sozo*—God's peace, shalom, protection, wholeness. Jesus didn't come to condemn us, but to offer us God's wholeness. And he never said we needed to accept his death in order for us to have this wholeness. In fact, as discussed in an earlier chapter, the word in John 3:16 for gave is in reference to a gift. A better translation of John 3:16 would be, "God so loved the world that he gifted his only Son." God's gift to us is the kind of life God lives— one of love, sacrifice, and service. The true gift of God is that God came to serve us and not to be served. This kind of life of selfless service is the example we are to follow, not one of death on a cross.

One more text to consider in John is 10:11, "I am the good shepherd. The good shepherd lays down his life for the sheep." This seems to indicate that Jesus came to die for us, the sheep. But we must look at this from the illustration itself. What good is a dead shepherd to the sheep? A dead shepherd cannot offer protection to the sheep from ravenous wolves. And remember, the meaning of salvation is *sozo*, or God's protection. We make an assumption of the text that it means Jesus offers us protection from God's wrath, but John does not indicate God is a wrathful god. John has gone to great lengths to paint Jesus as the image of God on the earth, one who loves the sheep and offers them protection from the evil of the world.

Look at John 12:31–32: "Now is the judgment of this world; now the ruler of this world will be driven out. And I, when I am lifted up from the earth, will draw all people to myself." The judgment is that Jesus showed the way of God's love, which is in direct opposition to the ruler of this world, a world filled with violence, death, and darkness. The lifting up of Jesus is not on the cross, but his return to God. His example of a life lived in God's perfect love and service draws people to God. His ascension also brings with it an assurance that we too will return to God. John, out of all the gospels, makes very clear that the gospel

---

7. It is interesting that Paul said in Romans 3:23, "all have sinned and fall short of the glory of God," but Jesus is not recorded as saying anything like this. Paul wrote Romans two to fifteen years before the gospel of Mark and twenty to thirty years before John wrote his gospel. Why is it that the gospel writers do not seem influenced by Paul's letters, particularly on the issue of atonement? It is a question to ponder.

message is about Jesus's life. So where does this preoccupation with the death of Jesus come from? I believe it is from Paul.

PAUL

As we begin to look at the letters of Paul, I want to point out that I will not cover all of Paul's letters, but just those passages that relate to atonement. Before we begin, I think it would be beneficial to have a general understanding about the person of Paul. He had a strong apocalyptic view. This means he believed in the imminent return of Jesus, which in the words of Raymond Brown, "does not encourage long-range social planning."[8] In other words, Paul was driven by his belief that Jesus would return in his lifetime. Couple this with his apparent need to be the best at everything, as evidenced in his letter to the Philippians where he says he was a Hebrew born of Hebrews and "as to righteousness under the law, blameless" (Phil 3:5–6), and you get a man hell-bent on a mission to convert everyone to Christ!

So it is no wonder that in Paul's earliest letter in the New Testament, I Thessalonians, written around 50 CE, some twenty years after the death and resurrection of Jesus, Paul commends the Thessalonians for turning from idols to serve God and "wait for his Son from heaven, whom he raised from the dead—Jesus, who rescues us from the wrath that is coming" (I Thess 1:10). In Paul's mind, the wrath that was coming was not far off, definitely not coming thousands of years later. This is why he encourages people to be like him and not marry (I Cor 7:8). Even to virgins he shares his opinion to remain single "in view of the impending crisis" (I Cor 7:26). This is why Paul is able to say that if you are a slave, remain in whatever condition you were in when called by God (I Cor 7:24), while also saying in Christ there is no slave or free (Gal 3:28).

For Paul, Jesus is returning soon, so endure your situation for a little while, because it's about to all change when Jesus returns and destroys every ruler, power, and authority, putting them under his feet, including death (I Cor 15:24–26). If we can grasp that this is Paul's state of mind, you can really empathize with him and understand where he is coming from when we look at his view of atonement. Paul really believed

---

8. Brown, *Introduction to the N.T.*, 506.

Jesus was coming back and wiping out all evil to establish God's way on the earth while he was still alive. Making sure you were forgiven and ready for Jesus was nothing to put on the back burner. "Get your life in order now" was Paul's position.

Not only did Paul not have time for people to act irresponsibly, he also did not have time for people to stand in his way of communicating the gospel. He had a deep conviction that he must do whatever was necessary for people to know the deep love of God revealed in Christ. Raymond Brown says Paul's most basic argument was this: "They [people] had to become aware of the love manifested by God in Christ, and nothing must be allowed to stand in the way."[9] Essentially, the same love that propelled Jesus now propelled Paul. And the source of that love was God. How can someone who is so filled with God's love also write that God is vengeful and bringing wrath?

I believe the answer to this question resides in his Jewish study of the law and commitment as a Pharisee before his conversion to Christ. Scholars believe Paul had relatives who lived in Jerusalem (Acts 23:16), so a young Paul in his 20s left Tarsus and headed to Jerusalem to study the law.[10] Paul took his study of the Jewish law and his Jewish heritage very seriously. By his own words, he was an Israelite; from the tribe of Benjamin, a distinction he shared with Saul, the first king of Israel and his namesake; a Hebrew born of Hebrews; and as to the law, a Pharisee (Phil 3:5). With his legal background, Paul approached God's righteousness "as if people were being brought before God for judgment and God is acquitting them and thus manifesting divine graciousness."[11] Paul had become a slave to the law, and his encounter with divine love in Christ on the road to Damascus truly was freedom from the law for him.

So when Paul says in Galatians 1:4 and 2:20 that Christ gave himself up for our sins, he truly means that Jesus set us free from the requirements of the law, the law that brings death (Rom 4:15, Rom 7:10, II Cor 3:6). Stoning to death was a common occurrence for breaking certain Jewish laws, and even Paul was subjected to this in Acts 14:19.

---

9. Brown, *Introduction to the N.T.,* 449.

10. Brown, *Introduction to the N.T.,* 426.

11. Brown, *Introduction to the N.T.,* 577.

Christ's death on a cross was a literal taking the place of anyone of Jewish descent, including Paul, who broke the law. For Paul, Jesus was a substitute in his atonement. But what about the Gentiles? How are they to be incorporated into God's great love? Jesus did not need to die for them. They were not Jewish and so they did not follow the Jewish law.

Paul carefully makes his argument in Galatians 2:15 that Gentiles are saved by faith in Christ, just like Israel. And he grounds saving faith all the way back to the father of Judaism, Abraham (Gal 3:6). Paul masterfully brings salvation through the death of Jesus to both the Jews and the Gentiles. In I Corinthians 15:21–22, Paul ties sin and death to Adam, as the first human being to sin, and true life for all to Christ. In this way, he can again bring the Gentiles into the Israelite history and story of God and tie them to faith in Christ and God's love for all the world. He repeats the Adam and Christ combination in Romans 5:12–21.

Romans has the most to say about atonement, particularly Romans 3:25–26, in which Paul notes that Jesus was a "propitiation" for sin. Remember, propitiation is to appease a god or spirit or person. This definitely supports the idea of substitutionary atonement heralded by Paul. But the actual Greek word Paul uses that we translate as propitiation is mercy seat. The mercy seat was the lid of the Ark of the Covenant that was sprinkled with blood from sacrificed animals on the Day of Atonement when the Jewish temple existed. Paul's reference here is an appeal to the Jewish followers of Jesus in the Roman church. The mercy seat would have little significance to Gentile followers of Jesus. His appeal is the same though—your sins are passed over through God's divine mercy for the one "who has the faith of Jesus" (Rom 3:26).

This verse can be translated "faith of Jesus" or "faith in Jesus." I believe a more accurate translation is faith of Jesus because it was Jesus's absolute trust in God that we are to emulate. Ultimately, it is this deep and abiding trust that we are forgiven that leads us to repentance and a joy-filled, Spirit-led life. Many of you may be wondering, "What is the purpose of your thesis that atonement is not necessary in understanding the death of Jesus if Paul proves that it is?" And this would be an excellent question. I am so happy you asked.

Paul's arguments are flawless and born of deep thinking, passion, and commitment to God's love in Christ for the world. But his reason for presenting Jesus as a substitutionary atoning sacrifice comes from his understanding of the Jewish law that brought death. Christians today, like the Gentiles of Paul's day, are not part of this world. Yes, sin is real in the world and we are all subject to it and its effects. But does that mean we need a substitute sacrifice to pay for this wrongdoing, inherited or not? I still would say, no.

As mentioned above, the gospel writers portrayed Jesus as bringing salvation through God's peace that surpasses all understanding. God's wholeness brought to us through Christ results in how we are to live in the world, how we are to treat and care for one another. I don't think Paul would disagree that a transformed life in Christ, where one is trying, with the help of God's Spirit, to live a life of love, is the goal. Paul's urgency in convincing people to follow God with the faith of Jesus came from his legal background and belief that the return of Jesus was imminent. So do we choose to follow the example of the gospels, or Paul?

I had lunch with a friend the other day. We were discussing my thesis and he asked, "Are you asking people to disregard Paul?" A great question! And the answer is no. Paul, like all the other writers of scripture, was inspired to write about God from his own place and time with his own gifts and many talents. Just as we are today. God inspires us through the writers of scripture and through the writing of others. In the modern world, we are inspired to love as God intends through music, movies, television, and people we have conversations with every day. The question is really what weight or authority do you place on scripture?

As I said at the beginning, I have a high view of scripture. God speaks to me through scripture and it is integral to my learning and understanding of God. But I also recognize that its writers were flawed like me. When Paul says in I Corinthians 14:34–35 that women should be silent in church, even if you believe Paul did not say this and it was added by an editor later, it is part of scripture. If you can overlook these verses and still have a vibrant faith in Jesus, can you not also overlook

Paul's desire to make Jesus's death substitutionary?

This does not make Paul's contribution to Christianity "less than." In the words of Raymond Brown, "Next to Jesus, Paul has been the most influential figure in the history of Christianity. . . . No Christian has been unaffected by what he has written."[12] In a very real way, Paul is a father to us all in the faith. We can love or hate Paul as many Christians do, but we cannot dismiss his contributions to the faith. Just as we may not like Paul's words that slaves should obey their masters, but love his words that love never fails, we can also not like his words that Jesus was a substitute for sin to spare us from God's wrath and still love his words that the fruit of the Spirit is love, joy, peace, patience, kindness, goodness, faithfulness, gentleness, and self-control.

OTHER BOOKS

The last two books in the New Testament that I wish to consider in our discussion about atonement are Hebrews and Revelation, particularly just two verses, Hebrews 9:22 and Revelation 5:9. Hebrews 9:22 says, "Indeed, under the law almost everything is purified with blood, and without the shedding of blood there is no forgiveness of sins." Almost all credible scholarship today does not believe that Paul wrote Hebrews. Yet, this verse in particular seems to follow Paul's thought on the substitutionary nature of God's forgiveness with the exception that the author of Hebrews offers in 9:24–28—Jesus as high priest, not just as a sacrifice. The author also offers that Jesus will come again to bring salvation.

The atonement that brings salvation in Hebrews is not like the gospel writers' view of salvation. It is not about life here and now. Nor is it like Paul's view of salvation, which is rescue from God's wrath. It is in the future and eagerly being awaited. The Greek word for "save" in verse 28 implies a physical and moral rescue. The author chooses not to focus on a wrathful God, but on an atoning sacrifice that brings a future of God's rest. Whereas Paul believed Jesus's return is imminent, the writer of Hebrews is dealing with a church that has begun to neglect doing good deeds and meeting together (10:24–25), perhaps because

---

12. Brown, *Introduction to the N.T.*, 422.

Jesus has not returned as soon as expected. Salvation is about waiting for something in the future. It is about holding on to faith and not losing hope.

This is a word for us today. As we await the return of Christ and God's end to evil, we cannot lose hope. It also means that we must continue to draw near to Christ and listen to the Holy Spirit as God moves and does new things. Letting go of sacrificial atonement images does not mean letting go of Jesus. The message of Jesus for us to repent, to genuinely be sorry for sin, and to work together with God to achieve God's kingdom on earth as it is in heaven, is the saving work we commit to with Christ. That doesn't change even if we stop believing in an atonement system. It can be a fresh new move of God's Spirit.

It was a new song that the angels sang in Revelation 5:9: "They sing a new song: 'You are worthy to take the scroll and to open its seals, for you were slaughtered and by your blood you ransomed for God saints from every tribe and language and people and nation.'" This new song sounds like an old song with its imagery of a slaughtered Jesus ransoming saints for God by his blood. The word for "ransom" used in this verse is in Greek the word "to buy," as if you are purchasing something from the market. There is no point in going over again what this language means in terms of atonement. What is worth noting is how this can be framed in view of God's love for humanity and the coming of God's way once and for all.

The slaughtered lamb represented by Jesus in this picture of the heavenly court, with angels singing and flying about, purchases humanity from the violence that has plagued the world for so long. This heavenly song of the sacrifice of Jesus can be reframed, not as an atonement for sin, but as God's redemption of humankind from every tribe, people group, and nation from the world's way of violence, intimidation, and evil. It is one of the "symbolic ways of predicting divine victory over evil forces that are an obstacle to God's kingdom or rule over the whole world."[13] God's will will be done. What Jesus came to put into motion will be fulfilled.

---

13. Brown, *Introduction to the N.T.*, 801.

Chapter 8
Can Atonement Views Be Damaging?

You have heard that it was said,
"You shall love your neighbor and hate your enemy."
But I say to you, love your enemies and pray for those who persecute you.
—Matthew 5:43–44

I hope that up to this point I have made a substantial case for getting rid of atonement views altogether. You don't have to agree with me, but I do hope we can agree that we do not wish to cause harm to others. The reality is that some atonement views are harmful. The majority of the harm centers on the idea that violence can be redemptive. When we say that God sent Jesus to die for our sins, we are condoning violence as a way to bring about good. This idea is called redemptive violence, and it fills our television and movie screens every day.

William Romanowski says that violence as a means of justice and making things right has a central place in American culture.[1] He uses one of my favorite movies, *The Matrix*, as an example. In the movie, the hero Neo becomes a Christ-like figure who sets out to set the people free who have been enslaved to live in a computer-generated virtual reality. In order to set them free, Neo enlists his partner Trinity to go with him, carrying "a duffel bag full of pistols, guns, and explosives needed to destroy the command center of political evil."[2] It really is a great movie, but it underscores the myth that violence sets us free from evil. Romanowski is not alone in the belief that we humans are addicted to violence as a way to end evil.

Walter Wink says that the myth of redemptive violence is a worldwide issue through national security systems.[3] It may seem strange to think of national security as an issue of atonement. Since atonement

1. Romanowski, *Eyes Wide Open*, 209.
2. Romanowski, *Eyes Wide Open*, 209.
3. Wink, *The Powers That Be*, 75.

is to repay for wrongdoing, there is no greater wrong that needs to be repaid then an attack on a nation's sovereignty. I remember 9/11 very well. I had not turned on the television or radio all morning as I was home preparing for a church-wide Bible study that evening. I took a break and walked the dog. As we were walking, we passed a house with some workmen outside. They had a radio on and I heard a newsperson talking about a plane flying into a building. I didn't hear the whole story, but had a sinking feeling. When we returned home, my phone was ringing and it was the senior pastor telling me he was canceling the Bible study for that evening. I asked why and he said, "Turn your television on, man! We are under attack!"

An attack on American soil. It was too much to believe. It wasn't long after that the Department of Homeland Security was formed, the War on Terror was declared, and we attacked Afghanistan to take out the Taliban. Violence leads to violence. A repayment had to be made and an assurance that more violence would not take place, and "the survival and welfare of the nation becomes the highest earthly and heavenly good."[4] I am not saying we should not have attacked the Taliban. In all honesty, I am glad I did not have to be the one to decide what our government's course of action should be. But we do have to be honest that redemptive violence is a part of our world.

In Matthew 26:52–53, when Jesus was praying in the garden of Gethsemane and then was betrayed into the hands of those who would eventually take his life, he told Peter to put down his sword, for those who live by the sword, die by the sword. He also refused to call down a multitude of angels to protect him. Jesus's refusal to buy into the world system of redemptive violence speaks to the power of nonviolence to bring about good. Had he not been crucified, his message of love, peace, and nonviolence would have continued in a dramatic fashion.

It is something to think about. What if Jesus had not been falsely found guilty and been released to go home to Capernaum? What would the world look like today? Or would Caiaphas's prediction have come true that the wrath of Rome would have come down on the small Jewish population (John 11:50)? Caiaphas's words that it is better for one man to die for the people than for the whole nation to perish are the

---

4. Wink, *The Powers That Be*, 56.

myth of redemptive violence in action. One act of violence against one man can redeem the whole nation from violence. The irony is that Jesus's death did not stop a Jewish uprising against Rome in 66 CE, which led to the destruction of the Jewish temple in 70 CE. Violence leads to violence.

Should the Jewish people have remained under oppressive Roman rule, or should they have fought for their freedom? Interestingly enough, Wink actually believes Jesus was teaching the people nonviolent resistance. For example, in Matthew 5:39b, when Jesus says to turn the other cheek if someone strikes you, it is assumed that you would be backhanded across the face because this type of strike is meant to humiliate someone who is inferior. By backhanding them, you are putting them back in their place. If you turn the other cheek, they would be forced to backhand you with the left hand. In the Jewish communities of Jesus's day, using the left hand was offensive because it was the hand one used for unclean purposes, like using the bathroom. It would be a cultural taboo to use the left hand, even for someone who viewed themselves as superior. The only way the person striking could hit you again would be with an open palm or fist. This type of slap or fist fight was for equals, not underlings. So by turning the other cheek, you were nonviolently resisting by saying, "I am your equal."[5]

Another of Jesus's teachings on nonviolent resistance is in the giving of the cloak if someone sues you and takes your coat (Matt 5:40). It is helpful to know the cultural context in order for this to be understood as a teaching on nonviolent resistance. According to Wink, "indebtedness was a plague in first-century Palestine."[6] This was not due to mismanagement of resources or a huge gap in wealth equity. Rome taxed the wealthy at a high percentage rate in order to fund its vast army. Owning land was the best way to hide wealth and avoid paying high taxes. Yet, land was passed down through generations, so it was not bought and sold with any frequency. But the wealthy could afford to offer high-interest loans to those who needed cash, often at 25 to 250 percent![7]

5. Wink, *The Powers That Be*, 101–2.
6. Wink, *The Powers That Be*, 103.
7. Wink, *The Powers That Be*, 104.

This would force landowners to sell their land to the wealthy in order to pay off high-interest loans. The rich kept getting richer at the expense of others. This practice is even mentioned in James 2:6: "But you have dishonored the poor. Is it not the rich who oppress you? Is it not they who drag you into court?" It was a Jewish legal practice to take someone's coat, but they were required to leave you with your undergarment and to return the coat at night so you would have something warm in which to sleep (Deut 24:10–13). Jesus is telling the poor person who is sued for his coat to give the wealthy person suing you the undergarment as well. While it was a shameful thing to be naked in public, it was considered more shameful to the wealthy person. As pointed out in Deuteronomy 24:13, the rich person would be giving up a blessing by taking the poor person's garments, and not receive credit before God.

Wink believes that Jesus was offering a nonviolent way for the Jewish people to begin liberating themselves, even before there was any kind of revolution, while recovering their humanity and dignity.[8] If Wink has correctly interpreted the cultural context and what Jesus was teaching the people, and I believe he has, then why would Jesus teach nonviolence all the while knowing that God was a violent god who required death as a payment for sin? I believe Jesus was revealing to us the character of God as one who is nonviolent and exposing the human propensity toward violence.

What about all the violence we see in scripture, especially the verses that attribute violence to God? Take, for instance, the well-known story of the walls of Jericho. God instructs Joshua to tell the people to take the sword of destruction to all the men and women, young and old, and all the oxen, sheep, and donkeys, except Rahab the prostitute and all her household because they protected the spies from Israel. I believe the writers of the Hebrew Bible were trying to communicate their understanding of God in a culture that did indeed capture cities and kill all its inhabitants. It doesn't mean God is violent. It means they were casting their violent ways upon God. They were trying to honor God as the one who delivered them from their enemies in the middle of a violent city takeover.

8. Wink, *The Powers That Be,* 109.

Just as we have examples of God and violence in scripture, we have examples of God and nonviolence in scripture. In *The Suffering of God: An Old Testament Perspective,* Terence Fretheim points out that in Isaiah 15:5, 16:9, 16:11 and in Jeremiah 48:30–32, 35–36 God moans, wails, and cries out for Moab. Fretheim says, "To hear such mourning on the part of God for a non-Israelite people is striking indeed. . . . [T]he impression created is that of a God whose lamentation is as deep and broad as that of the people themselves."[9] If every human being is created in the good image of God, then the loss of that image through death, especially a violent death, even of one's enemies, is a loss to God.

One of the greatest examples of the power of nonviolence to change oppressive systems is the civil rights movement in the United States. Rev. Martin Luther King Jr. was adamant that those protesting unjust and discriminatory laws against African Americans do so in a manner that was nonviolent. He received a lot of criticism for his position, but in the end it was television coverage of high-powered water hoses being turned on human beings and dogs attacking children as they marched nonviolently that changed the hearts of whites who contacted their legislators and asked for them to support civil rights legislation. At the heart of King's position were Jesus's words, "Love your enemies."

King said those who used physical force would be met with soul force; those who threw them in jail, would be met with love; those who committed hooded terrorism at night, beating civil rights supporters half dead, would be met with love. In his sermon on Matthew 5:43–45, King said, "One day we shall win freedom, but not only for ourselves. We will so appeal to your heart and conscience that we shall win you in the process, and our victory will be a double victory."[10] While chanting at a rally surrounded by Alabama state troopers, local police, and Sheriff Jim Clark, who had been one of the most vocal opponents of allowing black people the right to vote, a young black minister stepped up to the microphone and began singing "Do you love . . ." followed by the names of those who had been working to desegregate the south. And the crowd responded with, "Certainly, Lord!"

Then he said, "Do you love Sheriff Jim Clark?" And the people

9. Fretheim, *The Suffering of God,* 132–33.
10. King, *Strength to Love,* 51.

responded, "Certainly, Lord!" The Reverend James Bevel took the microphone and said, "It's not enough to defeat Jim Clark—do you hear me, Jim?—we want you converted. We cannot win by hating our oppressors. We have to love them into changing."[11] And Jim Clark did have a change of heart. But it took soul force and nonviolent love for that transformation to happen. Had the black communities that had been oppressed by whites for so long fought back against the violence perpetrated against them with violence, I do not think the hearts of men like Jim Clark would have changed.

A theology of atonement that uses violence to justify God's actions will only further violence among humanity. It will not bring about the type of change King's commitment to nonviolence was able to achieve in society and in individuals. Now let's look at a few individuals who actually did find atonement, substitutionary atonement to be precise, damaging.

Elizabeth Enns Petters is the daughter of Peter Enns, a professor of biblical studies at Eastern University and the host of the podcast *The Bible for Normal People.* In episode 77 of the podcast, titled "Anxiety in the Life of Faith," which aired on March 4, 2019, hosts Peter Enns and Jared Byas interviewed Peter's daughter on her experience of dealing with anxiety while growing up. She said:

> Coming from a conservative Christian home, I think a lot of what I was learning about God and faith and life was really fear-based. You know, accept Jesus or you're going to hell. Do this or you're punished. And so I think that from an early age I was sort of getting that message of fear. And I think it was coming from a lot of different directions, but in referencing my faith journey, I grew up with a fearful outlook of God.[12]

She goes on to say later in the podcast that she would pray to God as a teenager that she would be able to go to school as a tenth grader without having a panic attack. She prayed that God would make her a normal

---

11. Wink, *The Powers That Be,* 176–77.
12. Enns and Byas, "Anxiety in the Life of Faith," begins at 3:13.

teenager with a normal life "if he really loved me."[13]

Can views of atonement be damaging? The penal substitutionary view was for Elizabeth. It caused her to doubt God could love her and it led to severe anxiety that caused her family to seek professional help for her as early as age eight.[14] In the same podcast, host Jared Byas shared that his wife also suffered from anxiety. He said that in a conversation with his wife, they came to realize that the message of penal substitutionary atonement had also contributed to her anxiety, and that while some people may find the message that God punished Jesus for your sins as a motivator to be a changed person, different persons with different temperaments can "hear that same message and it can be paralyzing and terrifying for them."[15]

Anjelica Ruiz, whom we met in chapter six, converted to Judaism precisely because the fear-based atonement theology she had been taught as a child damaged her faith in God. She was told as a seven-year-old that she would go to hell if she did not believe in Jesus. When her grandmother died when she was ten years old, Ruiz became very angry at God, which is a perfectly understandable emotion to experience. But because of her upbringing, she felt extreme guilt for her grief and anger. She felt as though she would go to hell for doubting God's will in taking her grandmother. This hurt eventually led her to leave the Christian church altogether. It was not until she began researching Judaism, and began attending temple, that she discovered a sense of community based on love, not fear. She felt safe again in a place of worship and began the process of repairing her relationship with God.[16]

As Jared mentioned in the podcast *The Bible for Normal People* above, not all people are damaged from views of atonement. Obviously, it is the more punitive views that have the most capacity for harming people. But as I have wrestled with the issue of atonement, both the substitutionary views and the at-one-ment views, I do not find them helpful in explaining why Jesus had to die. If Jesus came to truly show us a better way of nonviolence and reveal to us a God of love, then I advocate for getting rid of atonement views altogether. If the goal of

---

13. Enns and Byas, "Anxiety in the Life of Faith," begins at 6:56.
14. Enns and Byas, "Anxiety in the Life of Faith," begins at 4:09.
15. Enns and Byas, "Anxiety in the Life of Faith," begins at 8:00.
16. Ruiz, in discussion with author, March 8, 2019.

the gospel is to communicate and live out God's will on earth as it is in heaven, and God's will is one where there are no more tears, no more death, but only love and perfect communion with God and one another, then why not communicate that? The only reason to mention violence and death is to say, "These are not God's way and God will end them both once and for all."

Lastly, I have a good friend whose story is truly intriguing and inspirational to me. Kelly was not raised in a religious home. She has vague recollections of attending a church service once or twice with a friend while growing up when she would spend the night at their house. But God, religion, and the Bible were not talked about in her home. She grew up feeling loved and supported with a wonderful sense of self-respect. There were a couple of moments in her adult life when she had what she called spiritual experiences. For one, while traveling by car in a remote area, she had an accident that ejected her from the car. It took two hours for an ambulance to arrive. On the way to the hospital, she remembers having a feeling that God was with her. She felt a complete sense of peace and calm, and that everything was going to be okay.

Once she arrived at the hospital, her injuries were too extensive to stay there, so she was care-flighted to a larger hospital. Before the transport, a nurse asked if she could pray for Kelly. She said yes. When her vitals were checked before the flight, she was told her bleeding had unexplainably stopped. In spite of these amazing touches of God's love and grace, it was not until her marriage of twenty-two years ended that she felt a need to pray and pursue God. Three years later, she is thankful to God for a church where she feels accepted and loved and a group of Christian friends that are nurturing her in the faith.

I share Kelly's story because in a substitutionary view of atonement, her experiences with God would not have been possible prior to accepting Christ's substitution for her sins. God's assuring presence of peace and calm, and the feeling that everything would be okay are more in line with the God revealed by Jesus, a God who heals and is present with those who need it most, regardless of what they believe or do not believe about Jesus.

Chapter 9
Where Do We Go from Here?

He [Jesus] is the reflection of God's glory and
the exact imprint of God's very being.
—Hebrews 1:3a

When we began this journey, I mentioned my friend Aaron who grew up in a conservative evangelical church where substitutionary atonement was taught. He grew up believing Jesus had to die for his sins. As he began to deconstruct this idea, he realized he no longer believed it. But it had been a core part of his understanding of what the gospel meant. When he asked me the question, "What do you do with Jesus if the atonement is no longer necessary?" I said, "Keep him." Jesus is essential to the gospel message because his life, his willingness to go to the cross and submit himself to a violent death without retaliation, and then his resurrection, all point to God's kingdom.

In Luke 17:20–21, when Jesus was asked when the kingdom of God would come, he replied, "The coming of the kingdom of God is not something that can be observed, nor will people say, 'Here it is,' or 'There it is,' because the kingdom of God is in your midst." The kingdom of God is not a physical place. It is a state of being. It's a way of living and being in the world that has compassion and empathy for others, cares for creation, loves God and others, and works toward healing and wholeness for all of creation, including people.

I also believe that the kingdom of God will be an actual point in time when God will come to dwell for all eternity on earth with humanity. At this point, time will cease to have meaning, because we will dwell with God for eternity. This dwelling with God will be a restoration of the Garden of Eden, where God walks with us in the cool of the evening breeze and asks us about our day (Gen 3:8). I long for this day! But in the meantime, we have the work of Jesus to do.

We need to be examples of nonviolent resistance against all forms of evil. We need to promote peaceful resolutions in situations of discord. In short, we need "to be conformed to the image of his Son, in order that he might be the firstborn within a large family" (Rom 8.29). And that really is it. Jesus came to remind us we are family, all with the same Father—God. I know referring to God as Father can be painful for some. I once served in a church where I had a member approach me after I prayed in the name of the Father. She said she grew up in a home with an abusive, alcoholic father, and for that reason she could not address God as Father and asked if I would be sensitive to this during my time at the church.

I honored her wishes and since then have addressed God only as God, and not Father. Certainly, God is the perfect parent and we can redeem hurtful images of earthly fathers who have harmed us. But I also think as we learn and grow in our faith understanding, we recognize that both male and female and those who are gender neutral are all created in the good image of God. So if it is helpful to others that we not identify God as masculine, I think that is part of the love Jesus is inviting us to show our neighbors. This is part of the conversation of where we go from here after leaving atonement behind. We are all family, so let's respect one another.

Paul really understood this, regardless of whether he missed the boat on atonement (see chapter 7 if you are reading this book backward). When writing to the church in Corinth, Paul addresses an issue they must have been dealing with—eating meat that had been sacrificed to idols. Some saw this as being wrong and something that should not be done. Others were like, "Eh, the idols aren't real gods. Why let good meat go to waste?" Paul said to take our brothers and sisters into consideration and not harm their faith by continuing to eat meat sacrificed to idols in their presence. In other words, out of love for your family, don't do it. For doing it unto them is doing it unto Christ (I Cor 8:12).

Family. It can be a wonderful life-giving thing, or it can be scarring and something you can't wait to get away from. Walter Wink says that the human family is "the most basic instrument of nurture, social control, enculturation, and training" in society.[1] Yet, Jesus consistently

1. Wink, *The Powers That Be*, 75.

critiqued the family and said that he came to divide families where sons and daughters would be against their parents and their parents against their children (Luke 12:51–53). Wink concludes that Jesus's critique was of the fallen human family and that Jesus came to restore the human family, not as a patriarchal unit of male, female, and children, but as one in which God is the perfect parent of all humanity.[2]

Wink supports this claim with Jesus' deliberate omission of father in Mark 3:35, "Whoever does the will of God is my brother and sister and mother," and in Mark 10:29–30, "There is no one who has left house or brothers or sisters or mother or father or children or fields . . . who will not receive a hundredfold now in this time—houses and brothers and sisters and mothers and children and lands." One can leave their earthly father but they do not receive a new father in the hundredfold blessing, for in the new family God is creating "you have one Father—the one in heaven" (Matt 23:9). The hundredfold blessing is the kingdom of God, the blessing is where God is our perfect parent and the rest of us are God's children—one big, happy, family.

Wink really drives home that, because societies are so heavily patriarchal, fathers must be eliminated to subvert the broken power structure—"no one can . . . claim the authority of the father, because that power belongs to God alone."[3] With God as the restored head of the new family created in Christ, proper relating to one another in love can take place. It is the answer to "Where do we go from here?" Get rid of atonement. Jesus didn't need to die to create a family for God. What Jesus did was model for us what loving others into a large family looks like. You might be thinking, "That sounds an awful lot like the Moral Influence Theory of atonement."

You would be correct. But the focus of atonement theories, either substitutional or example, are all about the death of Jesus. The message of Jesus was that God is the God of the *living*. God is a God of life, not death. The example Jesus showed us is about *living*. "I appeal to you therefore, brothers and sisters [my family], by the mercies of God, to present your bodies as a *living* sacrifice . . . ." (Rom 12:1, *emphasis mine*). How do we live with those who disagree with us? Isn't that the

2. Wink, *The Powers That Be*, 77.
3. Wink, *The Powers That Be*, 77.

challenge of every family in some way? In our cultural context, the issue that seems to be challenging our ability to live as an example of loving one another is the issue of homosexuality.

This is a crucial question. Whether you believe homosexuality is a sin or not, I believe Jesus is calling us to ask the question, "Did you do it unto me?" I served for two years on the board of an organization called Outlast Youth. The founder, Josh Cogan, was a Southern Baptist church planter. He felt called to plant a church in the Deep Ellum area of Dallas, Texas. It's kind of an artsy area that is currently going through a revitalization. Josh was struck by the number of homeless teenagers he kept running into who identified as LGBTQ. What he discovered as he began to research the issue was that 25 to 40 percent of homeless youth who identified as LGBTQ had been kicked out of conservative Christian homes because they were gay.

The message of Outlast Youth is, "No child deserves to be homeless." We can disagree about the theology surrounding homosexuality, but don't kick your children out. What we believe about God can cause harm to others, whether it is of a violent God who needs payment for sin, or of a God who hates gay people. Where do we go from here? I hope it is toward the kingdom of God where all people are loved and welcomed.

Let's face it, being a Christian doesn't make you a good person. Following any religion doesn't make you a good person. The kingdom of God isn't about being a good person. It's about having compassion and empathy for others because we are all bad people sometimes. We are all in this together. One night, I was feeling rather bitter toward someone who I felt wronged me. If you are familiar with the Enneagram personality profile, I'm a One. Resentment is the core weakness of a One. I was feeling resentful toward someone. Writing a book about the need to get rid of atonement, which is about repayment for wrongs committed, will mess with your mind. It suddenly dawned on me. The person who I felt wronged me didn't owe me anything. Jesus in his parable about the servant who is forgiven a great debt, then goes and has a person who owes him pennies thrown into jail, tells that parable to prove a point (Matt 18:21–35). Forgive as God forgives.

God doesn't hold grudges. God doesn't resent us when we screw up. God's not looking for good people. God knows us, faults and all. God is looking for people who realize we all mess up and therefore have humility, compassion, empathy, and forgiveness for others. I started a practice that night. When I feel resentment toward someone, I say to myself, "I am _____" and I insert that person's name. Try it. Think of someone who has hurt you or harmed you in some way. Say, "I am _____" and insert their name. This practice has helped remind me that we all sin. And Jesus's coming wasn't to wash away our sin so that we could be perfect. He was showing us that God knows us. God understands us. And God forgives us and has mercy on us. God causes the sun to shine on the righteous and the unrighteous.

That's the reason we don't give up on Jesus while letting go of atonement theories. Jesus is one of us. Jesus is with us in the good and the bad. He is with us when we screw up and when we do something really, really good. He is our brother, the firstborn of a large family, a family we are a part of. So where do we go from here? We do our best. We're not perfect. And we won't be until God finally refines us and makes us new once and for all. But we keep growing and learning to love like Jesus loved. We keep touching the hand of the one who needs to be touched because no one else will.

I mentioned Mark 3:1–6 earlier. It is the story of Jesus entering the temple and there is a man there with a shriveled hand. Jesus is being watched by the religious leaders to see if he will break the law and heal the man. Jesus asks the man to come forward and he asks the religious leaders, "Is it lawful to do good or to do harm on the sabbath, to save life or to kill?" And they are silent. The text says Jesus looked at them with anger. I wonder what the eyes of an angry God of love staring me down look like? And then it says his heart was grieved. Grief is sadness filled with hurt when there is nothing you know you can do about a situation. Like death. Jesus's heart is grieved because their hearts are hard. Instead of loving this man who has a shriveled hand, they use him as a means to plot to destroy Jesus (verse 6).

I don't know who you relate to in that story, who you identify with, but both Jesus and Paul said the fulfillment of the law was to love one another. Salvation is living in love. It is what you were created for. And the answer to the question, why did Jesus have to die? The answer is he didn't. We killed him because our hearts were hard. Love heals shriveled hands. Hatred, a hard heart—sin—kills. No atonement theory is needed to explain this. We know just by picking up our smart phones to open Facebook and see a post about the latest school shooting.

Rev. Martin Luther King Jr. said it best when he noted that the empires of Alexander the Great, Caesar, Charlemagne, and even Napoleon were built with great military might and conquest. But Jesus started an empire, a kingdom, built not on military conquest, but on love. "It started with a small group of dedicated men who, through the inspiration of their Lord, were able to shake the hinges from the gates of the Roman Empire and carry the gospel into all the world."[4] And Jesus's empire of love is still growing.

---

4. King, *Strength to Love*, 51.

Acknowledgments

I would like to thank Dr. Aaron Brown for looking at early drafts of this book and giving me positive and helpful feedback. I also would like to thank Aaron Manes, my spiritual director, for many conversations about theology in general and atonement specifically. Thank you to Dr. Elaine Heath, my mentor and friend, who offered words of support and encouragement during this process. There is not enough thanks in the world for the most amazing editor to grace the earth, without whom this book would be a mess—you know who you are! Thank you Matthew Vines for letting me bounce ideas off of you! And last but not least, thank you to Matthew Wimer, Editorial Production Manager at Wipf and Stock Publishers, for guiding me through this process and taking a chance on me.

Bibliography

Andrade, Gabriel. "René Girard (1923–2015)." In *Internet Encyclopedia of Philosophy: A Peer Reviewed Academic Resource.* https://www.iep.utm.edu/girard/#H1.

Baker, Sharon L. *Razing Hell: Rethinking Everything You've Been Taught about God's Wrath and Judgment.* Louisville, KY: Westminster John Knox, 2010.

Bass, Diana Butler. *Christianity after Religion: The End of Church and the Birth of a New Spiritual Awakening.* New York: HarperCollins, 2013.

Beilby, James, and Paul R. Eddy, eds. *The Nature of the Atonement: Four Views.* Downers Grove, IL: InterVarsity, 2006.

Bell, Rob. *Velvet Elvis: Repainting the Christian Faith.* Grand Rapids: Zondervan, 2005.

Brown, Brené. "January 21, 2018: (HD) Sunday Sermon by Dr. Brené Brown at Washington National Cathedral." Washington National Cathedral video, 17:51, January 21, 2018. https://www.youtube.com/watch?v=ndP1XDskXHY.

Brown, Raymond. *An Introduction to the New Testament.* New York: Doubleday, 1997.

Byas, Jared, and Peter Enns. "Anxiety in the Life of Faith." Interview with Elizabeth Enns Petters. *The Bible for Normal People* audio blog, March 4, 2019. https://peteenns.com/anxiety-in-the-life-of-faith.

Carey, Greg. "Luke's Interpretation of Jesus' Death." *HuffPost,* published March 22, 2016, updated March 23, 2017. https://www.huffpost.com/entry/lukes-interpretation-of-jesus-death_b_9517668.

Chase, Alexis. "3/15/15—4th Sunday in Lent." http://www.holycomforter-atlanta.org/uploads/5/4/3/6/54362277/3.15.15.pdf.

Enns, Peter. *How the Bible Actually Works.* New York: HarperCollins, 2019.

Fretheim, Terence. *The Suffering of God: An Old Testament Perspective.* Philadelphia: Fortress, 1984.

Green, Joel B. "Kaleidoscopic View." In *The Nature of the Atonement: Four Views,* edited by James Beilby and Paul R. Eddy, 157–85. Downers Grove, IL: InterVarsity, 2006.

Harper, Douglas. "Word Origin and History for Atonement." In *Online Etymology Dictionary* (2010). https://www.etymonline.com/search?q=atonement.

Hartke, Austen. *Transforming: The Bible and the Lives of Transgender Christians.* Louisville, KY: Westminster John Knox, 2018.

Heim, S. Mark. *Saved from Sacrifice: A Theology of the Cross.* Grand Rapids: Eerdmans, 2006.

Julian. *Revelations of Divine Love.* London: Penguin, 1998.

Keesmaat, Sylvia C., and Brian J. Walsh. *Romans Disarmed: Resisting Empire/ Demanding Justice.* Grand Rapids: Brazos, 2019.

King, Martin L. *Strength to Love.* Minneapolis: Fortress, 2010.

Kinnaman, David, and Gabe Lyons. *Unchristian: What a New Generation Really Thinks about Christianity . . . and Why It Matters.* Grand Rapids: Baker, 2012.

LaCugna, Catherine Mowry. *Freeing Theology: The Essentials of Theology in Feminist Perspective.* San Francisco: HarperSanFrancisco, 1993.

Lee, Justin. *Talking Across the Divide.* New York: TarcherPerigee, 2018.

Martyr, Justin. "Dialogue with Trypho." In *The Ante-Nicene Fathers,* edited by Alexander Roberts et al., vol. 1, 304-443. 1885; reprint, Grand Rapids: Eerdmans, 1993.

McHargue, Mike. *Finding God in the Waves: How I Lost My Faith and Found It Again through Science.* New York: Convergent, 2017.

Miller, Donald. *Building a Story Brand: Clarify Your Message So Customers Will Listen.* Nashville: Harpercollins Leadership, 2017.

Murphy, Caryle. "Most Americans Believe in Heaven . . . and Hell." Pew Research Center, published November 10, 2015. http://www.pewresearch.org/fact-tank/2015/11/10/most-americans-believe-in-heaven-and-hell/.

Onuma, Yasuaki. "Hugo Grotius: Dutch Statesman and Scholar." In *Encyclopedia Britannica Online,* April 6, 2019. https://www.britannica.com/biography/Hugo-Grotius.

Romanowski, William D. *Eyes Wide Open: Looking for God in Popular Culture.* Grand Rapids: Brazos, 2007.

Ruiz, Anjelica. Interview by author. Temple Emanu-El in Dallas, Texas. March 8, 2019.

Sanders, John, ed. *Atonement and Violence: A Theological Conversation.* Nashville: Abingdon, 2006.

Shadyac, Tom, writer and director. *I Am* DVD. Louisville, CO: Shady Acres, 2011.

Thompson, Marianne Meye. "Christus Victor: The Salvation of God and the Cross of Christ." *Fuller Studio* (2019). https://fullerstudio.fuller.edu/christus-victor-the-salvation-of-god-and-the-cross-of-christ.

Webb, Sean. *Mind Hacking Happiness.* Middletown, DE: CCRSM, 2017.

Wink, Walter. *The Powers that Be: Theology for a New Millennium.* New York: Galilee DoubleDay, 1998.